Betty Crocker's
All-Time
Favorites

Golden Press / New York
Western Publishing Company, Inc.
Racine, Wisconsin

Photography Director: LEN WEISS

REVISED EDITION
with recipes selected from the original edition

Second Printing This Format, 1985

Printed in the U.S.A. by Western Publishing Company, Inc.
Published by Golden Press, New York, New York.
Library of Congress Catalog Card Number: 70-165014

Golden® and Golden Press® are trademarks of Western Publishing Company, Inc.

ISBN 0-307-09938-5

Contents

All-Time Favorites...

If anything could please us more than the recipes in this collection, it's the number of good friends we've made through the years. There are the Betty Crocker home economists who have developed and perfected our recipes. The home testers who have double-checked them. And you, of course — the people who use our recipes day after day, year after year, and take the time to let us know how you like them. Only with this help were we able to bring you our personal collection of all-time favorites.

You might say that work on this book began in the 1920s, when some of these recipes, like Easy Oatmeal Bread and Golden Corn Pudding, were developed. It was back in those days, too, that we initiated our kitchen testing program. Later, kitchen testing was supplemented by home testing, ensuring the famous "Betty Crocker difference" — the knowledge that if you follow the recipes exactly, you can be sure of perfect results.

Today we do our kitchen testing in seven colorful, modern kitchens, which thousands of visitors tour every year. Here we answer an average of 4,000 letters and 3,000 phone calls each month. And here, of course, we also compile our cookbooks. Over the years we have created and developed, selected and perfected more than 22,000 recipes — a collection we like to think of as America's best recipes. Thus, the task of choosing the ones for this book was by no means an easy one. But thanks to what thousands of consumers and our own home economists have told us over the years, we made our selections. We hope you'll find many of your own all-time favorites on the pages that follow.

Meats and Main Dishes

SWEDISH MEATBALLS

1 pound ground beef
½ pound ground lean pork
½ cup minced onion
¾ cup dry bread crumbs
1 tablespoon snipped parsley
2 teaspoons salt
⅛ teaspoon pepper
1 teaspoon Worcestershire sauce
1 egg
½ cup milk
¼ cup salad oil
¼ cup all-purpose flour
1 teaspoon paprika
½ teaspoon salt
⅛ teaspoon pepper
2 cups water
¾ cup dairy sour cream

Mix thoroughly beef, pork, onion, bread crumbs, parsley, 2 teaspoons salt, ⅛ teaspoon pepper, the Worcestershire sauce, egg and milk.

Shape the mixture by rounded tablespoonfuls into small balls (about the size of walnuts). Heat salad oil in a large skillet and slowly brown and cook meatballs until they're done. Remove the meatballs from the skillet and keep warm.

Blend flour, paprika, ½ teaspoon salt and ⅛ teaspoon pepper into the oil in the skillet. Cook over low heat, stirring until the mixture is smooth and bubbly.

Stir in water and heat to boiling, stirring constantly. Boil and stir 1 minute.

Reduce heat and gradually stir in sour cream, mixing until smooth. Add meatballs; heat through.

6 to 8 SERVINGS.

BAKED MEATBALLS

1 pound ground beef
⅓ cup chopped onion
½ cup dry bread crumbs
1 teaspoon salt
⅛ teaspoon pepper
½ teaspoon Worcestershire sauce
1 egg
¼ cup milk

Heat oven to 400°. Mix all the ingredients thoroughly and shape the mixture into 1-inch balls. (Use a small ice cream scoop if you have one. It's a timesaver — and it makes meatballs of uniform size.)

Place the meatballs in an ungreased jelly roll pan, 15½ x 10½ x 1 inch. Bake 10 minutes or until done.

4 to 6 SERVINGS.

Pictured on the preceding page:
Chicken-Sausage Pies,
Pork Roast with Onion Gravy

CHEESE-CRUSTED MEATBALL CASSEROLE

1 pound ground beef
¼ cup dry bread crumbs
⅔ cup chopped onion
2 teaspoons salt
    Dash of pepper
½ cup milk
2 tablespoons butter or margarine
⅓ cup chopped onion
¼ cup chopped green pepper
1 can (16 ounces) tomatoes
1 can (6 ounces) tomato paste
½ cup sliced pimiento-stuffed olives
¼ teaspoon pepper
¼ teaspoon garlic salt
⅛ teaspoon crushed red pepper or a
    pinch of cayenne red pepper
    Cheese Pastry (below)

Mix ground beef, bread crumbs, ⅔ cup onion, the salt, a dash of pepper and the milk. Shape the mixture into 20 meatballs. Melt butter in a large skillet and brown meatballs.

Push the meatballs to the side of the skillet and add ⅓ cup onion and the green pepper. Cook and stir until the vegetables are tender. Stir in tomatoes, tomato paste, olives, ¼ teaspoon pepper, the garlic salt and red pepper. Heat to boiling over medium heat. Reduce heat and keep warm while preparing the pastry.

Heat oven to 425°. Prepare Cheese Pastry. Pour the hot meat mixture into an ungreased baking dish, 8 x 8 x 2 inches. Cut slits in pastry; place over hot meat mixture and flute the edge. Bake 30 minutes.

6 SERVINGS.

Crust plus! This versatile cheese pastry and a touch of imagination can do wonders. Remember it for your next deep-dish apple pie or for a tasty topper on beef stew.

Or roll out, cut into strips and sprinkle with caraway seed, poppy seed or paprika; bake 8 to 10 minutes in a 450° oven. *Voilà!* Crisp cheese sticks to use as hors d'oeuvres or as crunchy accompaniments for a soup or salad.

CHEESE PASTRY

1 cup all-purpose flour*
½ teaspoon salt
½ cup shredded Cheddar cheese
⅓ cup plus 1 tablespoon shortening
2 to 3 tablespoons cold water

Measure flour, salt and cheese into a bowl. Cut in shortening thoroughly with a pastry blender. Sprinkle in the water, 1 tablespoon at a time, mixing until all flour is moistened and dough almost cleans the side of the bowl (1 to 2 teaspoons water can be added if needed).

Gather the dough into a ball; shape into a flattened round on a lightly floured cloth-covered board. Roll into a 10-inch square.

*If using self-rising flour, omit salt. Pie crusts made with self-rising flour differ in flavor and texture from those made with plain flour.

FIESTA TAMALE PIE

1 pound ground beef
¼ pound bulk pork sausage
1 small onion, chopped
1 clove garlic, minced
1 can (16 ounces) tomatoes
1 can (16 ounces) whole kernel corn, drained
20 to 24 pitted ripe olives
1½ teaspoons salt
2 to 3 teaspoons chili powder
1 cup cornmeal
1 cup milk
2 eggs, well beaten
1 cup shredded American cheese

Heat oven to 350°. In a large skillet, cook and stir ground beef, pork sausage, onion and garlic until meat is brown and onion is tender. Drain off fat. Stir in the tomatoes, corn, olives and seasonings and heat to boiling.

Pour into an ungreased baking dish, 8 x 8 x 2 or 11 x 7 x 1½ inches, or a 2-quart casserole. Mix cornmeal, milk and eggs and pour over meat mixture. Sprinkle the cheese on top and bake 50 to 60 minutes or until golden brown.

8 SERVINGS.

Note: The meat mixture can be prepared ahead of time and kept, covered, in the refrigerator.

STUFFED GREEN PEPPERS

6 large green peppers
5 cups boiling salted water
1 pound ground beef
2 tablespoons chopped onion
1 teaspoon salt
⅛ teaspoon garlic salt
1 cup cooked rice
1 can (15 ounces) tomato sauce

Heat oven to 350°. Cut a thin slice from the stem end of each pepper. Remove all seeds and membrane. Wash outside and inside. Cook peppers in the boiling salted water 5 minutes; drain.

Cook and stir ground beef and onion in a medium skillet until onion is tender. Drain off fat. Add the salt and garlic salt. Stir in rice and 1 cup of the tomato sauce and heat through.

Lightly stuff each pepper with ½ cup of the meat mixture. Stand upright in an ungreased baking pan, 8 x 8 x 2 inches. Pour the remaining tomato sauce over the peppers. Cover and bake 45 minutes. Uncover and bake 15 minutes longer.

6 SERVINGS.

QUICK VEGETABLE SOUP

1½ pounds ground beef
3 cups water
1 cup cut-up carrots
1 cup diced celery
1 cup cubed pared potatoes
2 medium onions, chopped
  (about 1 cup)
1 can (28 ounces) tomatoes
2 teaspoons salt
1 teaspoon bottled brown bouquet
  sauce
¼ teaspoon pepper
1 bay leaf
⅛ teaspoon basil

Cook and stir ground beef in a large saucepan until brown. Drain off fat. Stir in the remaining ingredients and heat to boiling. Reduce heat. Cover and simmer just until the vegetables are tender, about 20 minutes.

6 SERVINGS.

HAMBURGER STROGANOFF

3 pounds ground beef
3 medium onions, chopped
2 cloves garlic, minced
2 teaspoons salt
½ teaspoon pepper
2 cans (6 ounces each) sliced
  mushrooms, drained
3 cans (10¾ ounces each)
  condensed cream of chicken
  soup
3 cups dairy sour cream or
  unflavored yogurt
12 ounces noodles, cooked and
  drained
  Snipped parsley

Cook and stir ground beef, onion and garlic in a Dutch oven or large roasting pan until meat is brown and onion is tender. Spoon off excess fat. Stir in salt, pepper, mushrooms and soup and heat to boiling, stirring constantly. Reduce heat and simmer uncovered 10 minutes.

Gradually stir in the sour cream and heat through. (Do not allow the mixture to boil or cream may curdle.) Spoon meat mixture over hot noodles and sprinkle with parsley.

12 SERVINGS (⅔ CUP NOODLES AND 1 CUP MEAT MIXTURE PER SERVING).

DILLED POT ROAST

2 tablespoons flour
1 teaspoon salt
¼ teaspoon pepper
3-pound beef chuck pot roast
  (arm or blade)
1 tablespoon shortening
¼ cup water
1 tablespoon vinegar
1 teaspoon dill weed
6 small potatoes, pared
6 carrots, quartered
½ teaspoon salt
4 or 5 zucchini (about 1 pound),
  quartered
½ teaspoon salt
  Sour Cream Gravy (below)

Mix flour, 1 teaspoon salt and the pepper and rub on the meat. Melt shortening in a large skillet or Dutch oven and brown meat over medium heat. (For a rich, brown gravy, brown the meat slowly and thoroughly.)

Drain off fat and add water and vinegar. Sprinkle half the dill weed on meat; turn and sprinkle with the remaining dill weed. Cover and simmer until tender, 2½ to 3 hours, adding a little water if necessary.

About 1 hour before the end of the cooking time, add potatoes and carrots and sprinkle with ½ teaspoon salt. Cover and simmer 40 minutes.

Add zucchini and sprinkle with ½ teaspoon salt. Cover and simmer 20 minutes longer or until the vegetables are tender. Remove the meat and vegetables to a platter and keep warm while making Sour Cream Gravy.

6 SERVINGS.

SOUR CREAM GRAVY

Measure the meat broth remaining in skillet; if necessary, add enough water to measure 1 cup. Mix 1 cup dairy sour cream, 1 tablespoon flour and 1 teaspoon dill weed in the skillet. Gradually stir in the meat broth and heat just to boiling, stirring constantly.

Dilled Pot Roast

BURGUNDY BEEF

3½ to 4 pounds beef round steak
    (top or bottom) or tip steak,
    1 inch thick
 ¼ cup shortening or bacon
    drippings
  5 large onions, sliced
  1 pound fresh mushrooms, sliced
  3 tablespoons flour
  2 teaspoons salt
 ¼ teaspoon marjoram
 ¼ teaspoon thyme
 ¼ teaspoon pepper
  1 cup beef bouillon*
  2 cups dry red wine

*Beef bouillon can be made by dissolving 1 beef bouillon cube or 1 teaspoon instant beef bouillon in 1 cup boiling water, or use canned beef broth.

Cut the meat into 1-inch cubes. Melt shortening in a Dutch oven and brown meat, about a third at a time, over medium heat. Remove meat and set aside.

Cook and stir onion and mushrooms in the Dutch oven until onion is tender, adding more shortening if necessary. Remove vegetables and set aside.

Return meat to the Dutch oven and sprinkle with flour and seasonings. Stir in bouillon and wine and heat to boiling. Lower the heat just enough to keep the mixture simmering. Cover and simmer until meat is tender, about 1¼ hours. Check once in a while to see that the liquid just covers the meat. If necessary, add more bouillon and wine (1 part bouillon to 2 parts wine). Add mushrooms and onion to the meat and heat through, stirring occasionally.

8 TO 12 SERVINGS.

OVEN-BARBECUED ROUND STEAK

3 pounds beef round steak (top
   or bottom) or tip steak,
   ¾ inch thick
2 tablespoons salad oil
½ cup chopped onion
¾ cup catsup
½ cup vinegar
¾ cup water
1 tablespoon brown sugar
1 tablespoon prepared mustard
1 tablespoon Worcestershire sauce
½ teaspoon salt
⅛ teaspoon pepper

Cut the meat into serving pieces. Heat oil in a large skillet and brown meat over medium heat, 15 to 20 minutes. Transfer the meat to an ungreased casserole. (You don't have to do this if your skillet is ovenproof.)

Mix the remaining ingredients and pour over the meat. Cover and cook in 325° oven until tender, 1½ to 2 hours.

8 TO 10 SERVINGS.

ROUND STEAK ROYALE

1½- to 2-pound beef round steak (top or bottom) or tip steak, ¾ inch thick
½ cup all-purpose flour*
1 teaspoon salt
1 teaspoon paprika
¼ teaspoon pepper
¼ cup shortening
1 can (4 ounces) mushroom stems and pieces, drained (reserve liquid)
1 large onion, sliced
½ cup dairy sour cream
¼ cup water

*If using self-rising flour, decrease salt to ½ teaspoon.

Cut the meat into serving pieces. Mix flour, salt, paprika and pepper; coat meat with the flour mixture. Melt shortening in a large skillet and brown meat over medium heat, 15 to 20 minutes. (If you like a rich, brown gravy, be sure to brown the meat slowly and thoroughly.)

Add enough water to the reserved mushroom liquid to measure ½ cup; pour into the skillet. Top meat with onion slices and mushrooms. Cover tightly and simmer until tender, 1½ to 2 hours, adding a little water if necessary.

Remove the meat to a warm platter. To make the gravy, stir sour cream and ¼ cup water into the skillet and heat *just* to boiling, stirring constantly.

6 SERVINGS.

ROUND STEAK WITH RICH GRAVY

3 pounds beef round steak (top or bottom) or tip steak, 1 inch thick
⅓ cup all-purpose flour
3 tablespoons shortening
1 envelope (about 1½ ounces) onion soup mix
½ cup water
1 can (10¾ ounces) condensed cream of mushroom soup

Sprinkle one side of the meat with half the flour and pound in. (Use a mallet or the edge of a heavy saucer.) Turn meat and pound in the remaining flour. Cut into serving pieces.

Melt shortening in a large skillet and brown meat slowly and thoroughly over medium heat, 15 to 20 minutes. Sprinkle onion soup mix over meat. Mix water and mushroom soup and pour over meat. Cover tightly and simmer until tender, 1½ to 2 hours, adding a little water if necessary.

Remove the meat to a warm platter. Heat the remaining gravy mixture to boiling, stirring constantly, and pour over the meat.

8 TO 10 SERVINGS.

CHINESE BEEF AND PEA PODS

1 - pound beef tenderloin or boneless sirloin steak, ¾ inch thick
1 tablespoon soy sauce
1 thin slice fresh gingerroot, crushed*
1 clove garlic, crushed*
1 package (6 ounces) frozen Chinese snow peas
¼ cup salad oil
¼ pound fresh mushrooms, sliced
3 stalks celery cabbage or bok choy, cut diagonally into ¼-inch slices (about 2 cups)
1 medium onion, sliced
½ can (8-ounce size) water chestnuts, drained and thinly sliced
1 can (8 ounces) bamboo shoots, drained
1 can (13¾ ounces) chicken broth (1⅔ cups)
3 tablespoons cornstarch
2 tablespoons soy sauce
½ teaspoon salt
¼ teaspoon sugar
  Chow mein noodles or hot cooked rice

*Place gingerroot and garlic between two pieces of waxed paper and crush with a wooden mallet.

Cut the meat across the grain into very thin slices. (You'll find it much easier to slice the meat if it's partially frozen — or ask your meatman to slice it for you.) Mix 1 tablespoon soy sauce, the gingerroot and garlic and sprinkle on meat; toss until meat is coated. For extra flavor, let marinate at least 30 minutes.

Place frozen snow peas in a colander or sieve and run cold water over pods just until they're separated. Drain.

Heat 2 tablespoons of the salad oil in a large skillet and brown meat over medium-high heat, turning once. Remove meat to a warm platter.

Add the remaining 2 tablespoons salad oil to the skillet and cook and stir mushrooms, cabbage, onion, water chestnuts and bamboo shoots over high heat 2 minutes. Stir in snow peas and 1 cup of the chicken broth. Cover and cook over medium heat 2 minutes.

Mix remaining chicken broth, the cornstarch, soy sauce, salt and sugar and pour into the skillet. Cook, stirring constantly, until the mixture thickens and boils. Boil and stir 1 minute. Add the meat and heat through. Serve over chow mein noodles.

5 SERVINGS.

HAM AND SPICED FRUITS

2 bananas, peeled and quartered
1 can (8 ounces) peach halves
1 can (8 ounces) pear halves
12 maraschino cherries, halved
¼ teaspoon pumpkin pie spice
2- to 3-pound canned* or fully cooked boneless smoked ham
4 to 6 medium sweet potatoes, cooked, peeled and halved, or 1 can (23 ounces) sweet potatoes, drained
1 cup brown sugar (packed)
1 teaspoon dry mustard

*Remove gelatin from canned ham before baking.

Combine bananas, peach halves (with syrup), pear halves (with syrup), cherries and pumpkin pie spice. Pour off ½ cup syrup and reserve for the glaze. Refrigerate the fruit.

Heat oven to 350°. Place ham in an ungreased baking dish, 11 x 7 x 1½ inches, and arrange sweet potato halves around ham. Mix brown sugar, reserved fruit syrup and dry mustard; pour over the ham and potatoes. Bake uncovered 1 hour, basting ham and potatoes with the syrup several times.

Drain the spiced fruits and arrange attractively on and around the ham. Bake uncovered until fruits are heated through, about 15 minutes.

6 TO 10 SERVINGS.

PORK ROAST WITH ONION GRAVY

1 envelope (about 1½ ounces) onion soup mix
5-pound pork loin roast
½ cup water
¼ cup all-purpose flour

We guarantee you've never tasted a pork roast as moist and delicious as this one. And it's so easy to make a smooth gravy with the rich drippings — if you remember to add the flour to the water, never the reverse. (With quick-mixing flour, it's even easier — just *stir* it in.)

Place a 30 x 18-inch piece of heavy-duty aluminum foil in a baking pan, 13 x 9 x 2 inches. Sprinkle soup mix in the center of foil. Trim excess fat from roast. Place roast fat side down on the soup mix. Fold foil over and seal securely, folding up the ends. Cook in 300° oven 3½ hours. Meat thermometer should register 170° when done.

Open the foil wrapping and remove the meat to a platter; keep warm while making the gravy. Skim excess fat from the meat drippings in the foil. Measure the drippings and add enough water to measure 2 cups. Pour into the pan.

Shake water and flour in a covered jar. Stir flour mixture slowly into liquid in the pan. Heat to boiling, stirring constantly. Boil and stir 1 minute.

8 TO 12 SERVINGS.

3¾ pounds pork shoulder
¾ cup all-purpose flour*
1 tablespoon plus 1 teaspoon
    ginger
½ cup salad oil
2 cans (15½ ounces each)
    pineapple chunks, drained
    (reserve syrup)
½ cup vinegar
½ cup soy sauce
1 tablespoon Worcestershire sauce
¾ cup sugar
1 tablespoon salt
¾ teaspoon pepper
2 small green peppers, cut into
    strips
1 can (16 ounces) bean sprouts,
    drained
1 can (8 ounces) water chestnuts,
    drained and thinly sliced
2 tablespoons chili sauce
    Easy Oven Rice (below)

*If using self-rising flour, decrease salt to 2¼ teaspoons.

SWEET 'N SOUR PORK

Cut the meat into 1-inch cubes, trimming off any excess fat. Mix half the flour with the ginger; coat meat thoroughly with the flour mixture. Heat oil in a large skillet or Dutch oven and brown meat, about a third at a time, over medium heat. Remove meat and set aside.

Add enough water to the reserved pineapple syrup to measure 1¾ cups and gradually stir into the remaining flour. Stir pineapple syrup mixture, vinegar, soy sauce and Worcestershire sauce into the fat in skillet.

Heat to boiling, stirring constantly. Boil and stir 1 minute. Stir in sugar, salt, pepper and meat. Reduce heat. Cover and simmer until the meat is tender, about 1 hour, stirring occasionally.

Add pineapple and green peppers and cook uncovered 10 minutes. Stir in bean sprouts, water chestnuts and chili sauce and heat through, about 5 minutes. Serve over the hot rice.

10 SERVINGS.

EASY OVEN RICE
4 cups boiling water
2 cups uncooked regular rice
2 teaspoons salt

Heat oven to 350°. Mix ingredients thoroughly in an ungreased 2-quart casserole or in a baking dish, 13 x 9 x 2 inches. Cover tightly. Bake 25 to 30 minutes or until the liquid is absorbed and the rice is tender.

6 CUPS COOKED RICE.

PORK CHOPS SUPREME

2 tablespoons shortening
6 pork loin or rib chops,
   ¾ to 1 inch thick
   Salt and pepper
6 thin onion slices
6 thin lemon slices
6 tablespoons brown sugar
6 tablespoons catsup

Melt shortening in a large skillet and brown chops over medium heat. Season chops with salt and pepper and place them in a shallow baking pan or baking dish. Top each chop with an onion slice, a lemon slice, 1 tablespoon brown sugar and 1 tablespoon catsup.

Cover and cook in a 350° oven 30 minutes. Uncover and cook until done, about 30 minutes longer — basting the chops occasionally.

6 SERVINGS.

Here's a great favorite with the guests in our dining room. The menu often features lemon broccoli, hot corn muffins and strawberry shortcake.

PORK CUTLETS MORNAY

6 pork sirloin cutlets
2 eggs, beaten
½ cup dry bread crumbs
¼ cup shortening or salad oil
2 tablespoons water
6 tablespoons tomato sauce or catsup
   Mornay Sauce (below)
½ cup shredded Cheddar cheese
   Paprika

Dip the cutlets in egg, then coat with bread crumbs. Melt shortening in a large skillet and brown meat over medium heat. Add water and reduce heat. Cover and cook over low heat until done, about 30 minutes.

Arrange meat in an ungreased baking dish, 13½ x 9 x 2 inches. Top each cutlet with 1 tablespoon tomato sauce. Spoon Mornay Sauce on meat and sprinkle with the cheese and paprika.

Set oven control at broil and/or 550°. Broil cutlets 6 to 7 inches from heat until cheese is melted and sauce is bubbly around edges.

6 SERVINGS.

MORNAY SAUCE

1 tablespoon butter or margarine
1 tablespoon flour
⅛ teaspoon each salt, nutmeg and cayenne red pepper
½ cup chicken broth*
½ cup half-and-half
½ cup shredded Cheddar cheese

Melt butter in a small saucepan. Blend in flour and seasonings. Cook over low heat, stirring constantly, until the mixture is smooth and bubbly. Immediately stir in chicken broth and half-and-half. Heat to boiling, stirring constantly. Boil and stir 1 minute. Stir in cheese until melted.

*Chicken broth can be made by dissolving ½ teaspoon instant chicken bouillon in ½ cup boiling water.

EGGPLANT PARMIGIANA

Italian Sauce (below)
1 medium eggplant (1¼ to 1½ pounds)
1 package (6 ounces) sliced mozzarella cheese (reserve 2 slices)
½ cup grated Parmesan cheese

Prepare Italian Sauce. Heat oven to 350°. Pare eggplant and cut into ¼-inch slices. Alternate layers of eggplant slices with mozzarella cheese slices and Italian Sauce in an ungreased 2-quart casserole. Sprinkle with Parmesan cheese and top with the reserved mozzarella.

Cover and bake 50 minutes. Uncover and bake 10 minutes longer or until the cheese is melted and light brown.

6 SERVINGS.

ITALIAN SAUCE
1 pound Italian or bulk pork sausage
1 can (16 ounces) tomatoes
1 can (6 ounces) tomato paste
1 clove garlic, minced
2 tablespoons snipped parsley
1 tablespoon minced onion
½ teaspoon salt
½ teaspoon oregano
¼ teaspoon pepper

Cook and stir sausage in a large skillet until brown. Drain off fat. Stir in the remaining ingredients. Cover and simmer 45 minutes.

3½ CUPS.

CHEESE STRATA

⅓ cup soft butter or margarine
1 clove garlic, crushed
½ teaspoon dry mustard
10 slices white bread, crusts
     removed
2 cups shredded sharp Cheddar
     cheese
2 tablespoons chopped onion
2 tablespoons snipped parsley
1 teaspoon salt
½ teaspoon Worcestershire sauce
⅛ teaspoon pepper
     Dash of cayenne red pepper
4 eggs
2⅓ cups milk
⅔ cup dry white wine*

*If you prefer, omit the wine and increase milk to
2½ cups.

Mix butter, garlic and mustard and spread on one side of each bread slice. Cut each slice into thirds. Line the bottom and sides of an ungreased baking dish, 8 x 8 x 2 inches, with some of the bread slices, buttered sides down.

Mix cheese, onion, parsley, salt, Worcestershire sauce, pepper and cayenne red pepper; spread evenly in the baking dish. Top with the remaining bread slices, buttered sides up. Beat eggs and blend in the milk and wine; pour over the bread. Cover and refrigerate at least 2 hours.

Heat oven to 325°. Bake uncovered until golden brown, about 1¼ hours. (To test, a knife inserted in center will come out clean.) Let stand 10 minutes before serving.

6 SERVINGS.

QUICHE LORRAINE

     Pastry for 9-inch One-crust Pie
     (page 76)
12 slices bacon (½ pound),
     crisply fried and crumbled
1 cup shredded natural Swiss
     cheese (about 4 ounces)
⅓ cup minced onion
4 eggs
2 cups whipping cream or half-
     and-half
¾ teaspoon salt
¼ teaspoon sugar
⅛ teaspoon cayenne red pepper

Heat oven to 425°. Prepare the pastry. Sprinkle bacon, cheese and onion in the pastry-lined pie pan. Beat eggs slightly and blend in the remaining ingredients. Pour into the pie pan.

Bake 15 minutes, then reduce the oven temperature to 300° and bake 30 minutes longer or until a knife inserted halfway between center and edge comes out clean. Let the pie stand 10 minutes before cutting. Serve in wedges.

6 MAIN-DISH OR 8 APPETIZER SERVINGS.

CHICKEN FRICASSEE WITH DUMPLINGS

4-pound stewing chicken, cut up
1 cup all-purpose flour*
2 teaspoons salt
2 teaspoons paprika
¼ teaspoon pepper
   Shortening or salad oil
1 cup water
3 tablespoons flour
   Milk
   Dumplings (below)

*If using self-rising flour, decrease salt to 1 teaspoon.

If you like, mix a couple of tablespoons of snipped chives or parsley into the dumpling batter. Or add a subtle boost of flavor to the simmering chicken broth instead — with sliced onions, celery tops, carrot slices or your favorite herbs.

Wash the chicken and pat dry. Mix 1 cup flour, the salt, paprika and pepper; coat chicken with the flour mixture. Heat a thin layer of shortening in a large skillet or Dutch oven and brown chicken over medium heat. Drain off fat and reserve.

Add water to the skillet. Cover and simmer until the chicken is fork-tender, 2½ to 3½ hours, adding more water if necessary. Remove the chicken and keep warm while making the gravy. Drain the liquid from skillet and reserve.

To make the gravy, heat 3 tablespoons of the reserved fat in skillet. Blend in 3 tablespoons flour. Cook over low heat, stirring until the mixture is smooth and bubbly. Remove from heat. Add enough milk to the reserved liquid to measure 3 cups and pour into the skillet. Heat to boiling, stirring constantly. Boil and stir 1 minute.

Return chicken to the gravy in the skillet. Prepare dough for Dumplings and drop by spoonfuls onto hot chicken. Cook uncovered 10 minutes. Cover and cook 20 minutes longer.

8 SERVINGS.

DUMPLINGS

1½ cups all-purpose flour**
  2 teaspoons baking powder
  ¾ teaspoon salt
  3 tablespoons shortening
  ¾ cup milk

Measure flour, baking powder and salt into a bowl. Cut in shortening thoroughly with a pastry blender until mixture looks like meal. Stir in the milk.

**If using self-rising flour, omit baking powder and salt.

Oven-fried Chicken

OVEN-FRIED CHICKEN

2½ to 3 pounds broiler-fryer
    chicken pieces
¼ cup shortening
¼ cup butter or margarine
½ cup all-purpose flour*
1 teaspoon salt
1 teaspoon paprika
¼ teaspoon pepper

*If using self-rising flour, decrease salt to ½ teaspoon.

Heat oven to 425°. Wash the chicken and pat dry. Melt shortening and butter in baking pan, 13 x 9 x 2 inches, in the oven.

Mix flour, salt, paprika and pepper; coat chicken thoroughly with the flour mixture. Place chicken skin side down in the pan. Bake uncovered 30 minutes. Turn the chicken and bake until thickest pieces are fork-tender, 20 to 30 minutes longer.

6 SERVINGS.

VARIATION

Crunchy Oven-fried Chicken: Substitute 3 cups corn puffs cereal, crushed, for the flour mixture. Roll chicken in the melted shortening and butter, then coat with the cereal.

ALMOND OVEN-FRIED CHICKEN

2 broiler-fryer chickens (2½
    pounds each), cut up
    Salt
2 tablespoons butter or margarine
2 tablespoons shortening
1 cup all-purpose flour*
2 teaspoons salt
2 teaspoons paprika
¼ teaspoon pepper
2 eggs, slightly beaten
3 tablespoons milk
2 cups finely chopped blanched
    almonds
¼ cup butter or margarine, melted

*If using self-rising flour, decrease the 2 teaspoons salt to 1 teaspoon.

Heat oven to 400°. Wash the chicken and pat dry. Remove skin from all pieces except the wings. Sprinkle chicken lightly with salt.

Melt 2 tablespoons butter and the shortening in a jelly roll pan, 15½ x 10½ x 1 inch, in the oven. Mix flour, 2 teaspoons salt, the paprika and pepper. Combine eggs and milk. Coat chicken with the flour mixture; dip into egg and milk and roll in nuts. Place chicken bone side down in the pan and drizzle with melted butter. Bake uncovered until thickest pieces are fork-tender, about 1 hour.

12 SERVINGS.

SHERRIED CHICKEN SUPREME

2 tablespoons butter or margarine
2 tablespoons salad oil
6 large chicken breast halves
(2½ to 3 pounds)
1 can (10¾ ounces) condensed
cream of chicken soup
½ cup half-and-half
½ cup dry sherry or, if desired,
½ cup apple juice plus 3
tablespoons sherry flavoring
1 can (15½ ounces) pineapple
chunks, drained
½ cup sliced seedless green grapes
1 can (6 ounces) sliced mushrooms,
drained

Heat oven to 350°. Heat butter and oil in a baking dish, 13½ x 9 x 2 inches. Place chicken pieces skin side up in the baking dish and bake uncovered 1 hour.

Heat soup, half-and-half and sherry in a saucepan, stirring occasionally. Stir in pineapple, grapes and mushrooms.

Remove the baking dish from the oven and drain off fat. Pour the soup mixture over chicken. Cover with aluminum foil and continue baking until chicken is fork-tender, 15 to 20 minutes longer. Garnish with clusters of seedless green grapes.

6 SERVINGS.

CHICKEN-WILD RICE CASSEROLE

½ cup butter or margarine
½ cup all-purpose flour*
2½ teaspoons salt
¼ teaspoon pepper
1½ cups chicken broth**
2¼ cups milk
2¼ cups cooked wild or white rice
3 cups cut-up cooked chicken
2 jars (4½ ounces each) sliced
mushrooms, drained
½ cup chopped green pepper
1 jar (2 ounces) sliced pimiento,
drained
⅓ cup slivered almonds
Snipped parsley

*If using self-rising flour, decrease salt to 2 teaspoons.

**Chicken broth can be made by dissolving 1½ teaspoons instant chicken bouillon in 1½ cups boiling water, or use canned chicken broth.

Heat oven to 350°. Melt butter in a large skillet or Dutch oven. Blend in flour, salt and pepper. Cook over low heat, stirring until mixture is smooth and bubbly. Immediately stir in chicken broth and milk. Heat to boiling, stirring constantly. Boil and stir 1 minute.

Stir in rice, chicken, mushrooms, green pepper, pimiento and almonds. Pour into a greased baking dish, 13½ x 9 x 2 inches. Bake 40 to 45 minutes. Sprinkle with parsley.

12 SERVINGS (3-INCH SQUARE PER PORTION).

VARIATION

Turkey-Wild Rice Casserole: Substitute 3 cups cut-up cooked turkey for the chicken.

CHICKEN-SAUSAGE PIES

½ pound bulk pork sausage
  Savory Pastry (below)
1 jar (2½ ounces) sliced mushrooms,
  drained (reserve liquid)
¼ cup butter or margarine
⅓ cup all-purpose flour
¼ teaspoon salt
1 can (13¾ ounces) chicken broth
  (1⅔ cups)
1 cup half-and-half
2 cups cut-up cooked chicken

Pretty up the pastry by making cross-slits or cutouts in the center. Or try one of our dining room favorites: old-fashioned Chicken Littles. Roll any leftover pastry about ¼ inch thick and cut with a small chicken-shaped cookie cutter (or trace around a pattern with a knife). Insert a wooden pick half-way into the base of each "chicken" and prick with a fork. Bake right along with the rounds, only keep these in the oven a bit longer — 10 to 15 minutes in all, or until golden brown. Then simply stand a Chicken Little upright in the center of each crust.

For a touch of color, garnish the pies with parsley and pimiento strips.

Heat oven to 400°. Shape pork sausage into ½-inch balls. Place on rack in broiler pan and bake 15 minutes. Remove from the oven and set aside.

Increase the oven temperature to 425°. Prepare Savory Pastry and place the pastry rounds on an ungreased baking sheet; prick thoroughly with a fork. Bake 8 to 10 minutes or until golden brown.

Cook and stir mushrooms in butter 5 minutes. Stir in flour and salt and cook over low heat, stirring until mixture is bubbly. Immediately stir in broth, half-and-half and the reserved liquid. Heat to boiling, stirring constantly. Boil and stir 1 minute.

Divide sausage balls and chicken among the 6 ungreased casseroles. Pour the cream sauce over meat. Top each casserole with a baked pastry round. Heat in 425° oven until the sauce bubbles.

6 SERVINGS.

SAVORY PASTRY
1 cup all-purpose flour*
1 teaspoon celery seed
½ teaspoon salt
½ teaspoon paprika
⅓ cup plus 1 tablespoon shortening
2 to 3 tablespoons cold water

Measure flour, celery seed, salt and paprika into a bowl. Cut in shortening thoroughly. Sprinkle in the water, 1 tablespoon at a time, mixing until dough almost cleans side of bowl. Gather the dough into a ball and shape into a flattened round. Roll about ⅛ inch thick on a lightly floured cloth-covered board. Cut into 6 rounds to fit the tops of 1½-cup individual casseroles.

*If using self-rising flour, omit salt.

HOT CHICKEN SUPPER SALAD

2 cups cut-up cooked chicken
2 cups thinly sliced celery
1 cup toasted bread cubes
1 cup mayonnaise
½ cup toasted slivered almonds
2 tablespoons lemon juice
¼ cup chopped onion
½ teaspoon salt
½ cup shredded Cheddar cheese
1 cup toasted bread cubes or
   crushed potato chips

Heat oven to 350°. Combine all ingredients except the cheese and 1 cup bread cubes. Pile into 4 or 5 ungreased individual casseroles or an ungreased 2-quart casserole. Sprinkle with cheese and bread cubes. Bake individual casseroles 20 to 25 minutes, 2-quart casserole 30 to 35 minutes or until hot and bubbly.

5 OR 6 SERVINGS.

VARIATION

Hot Tuna Supper Salad: Substitute 2 cans (6½ ounces each) tuna, drained, for the chicken.

CHICKEN CLUB SALAD

Barbecue Salad Dressing (below)
1 head lettuce, washed and chilled
8 to 10 slices bacon, crisply fried
2 cups cubed cooked chicken, chilled
2 large tomatoes, cut into eighths
1 hard-cooked egg, sliced

Prepare Barbecue Salad Dressing. Tear the lettuce into bite-size pieces (about 6 cups). Break bacon into large pieces.

Just before serving, add bacon and chicken to the lettuce and toss lightly. Garnish with tomato wedges and egg slices. Serve with the salad dressing.

4 SERVINGS.

BARBECUE SALAD DRESSING

½ cup mayonnaise or salad dressing
¼ cup barbecue sauce
1 tablespoon instant minced onion
1 tablespoon lemon juice
½ teaspoon salt
¼ teaspoon pepper

Blend all ingredients. Cover and refrigerate.

ABOUT ¾ CUP.

CHICKEN SALAD IN PINEAPPLE BOATS

2	pineapples
2½	cups cut-up cooked chicken or turkey
¾	cup diced celery
¾	cup mayonnaise or salad dressing
2	tablespoons chopped chutney
1	teaspoon curry powder
1	medium banana
⅓	cup salted peanuts
½	cup flaked coconut
1	can (11 ounces) mandarin orange segments, drained

Quarter each pineapple, cutting right through the green top. Remove fruit; core and cut into chunks. Drain the pineapple shells on paper towels.

Combine pineapple chunks, chicken and celery in a large bowl. For the dressing, mix mayonnaise, chutney and curry powder in another bowl. Cover both bowls and chill at least 1 hour.

Just before serving, drain the liquid from the chicken mixture. Slice banana into the bowl, then add peanuts and the dressing. Toss until all ingredients are well coated.

Spoon the salad into the pineapple shells and sprinkle each with coconut. Garnish with orange segments.

8 SERVINGS.

Chicken salad with a tropical touch. For "clear sailing," use a grapefruit knife to cut along the edge of the pineapple boat.

CREOLE FLOUNDER

2 pounds fresh or frozen flounder
  fillets
1½ cups chopped tomatoes
½ cup chopped green pepper
⅓ cup lemon juice
1 tablespoon salad oil
2 teaspoons salt
2 teaspoons minced onion
1 teaspoon basil leaves
¼ teaspoon coarsely ground black
  pepper
4 drops red pepper sauce

Thaw the fillets if they're frozen. Heat oven to 500°. Place fillets in a single layer in an ungreased baking dish, 13½ x 9 x 2 inches. Mix the remaining ingredients and spoon over fillets. Bake until fish flakes easily with a fork, 5 to 8 minutes. Remove fillets to a warm platter. Garnish with tomato wedges and green pepper rings.

8 SERVINGS.

CRABMEAT AVOCADO

4 ripe avocados
  Lemon juice
  Salt
1 can (2 ounces) mushroom stems
  and pieces, drained
2 tablespoons butter or margarine
2 tablespoons flour
1 teaspoon salt
¼ teaspoon white pepper
1 cup half-and-half
1 egg yolk, beaten
¼ cup chopped ripe olives
2 cans (7¾ ounces each) crabmeat,
  drained and cartilage removed
  Grated Parmesan cheese

Heat oven to 325°. Cut each unpeeled avocado in half. Brush with lemon juice (to prevent discoloration) and sprinkle with salt. Place in ½ inch of hot water in a baking dish, 13½ x 9 x 2 inches.

Cook and stir mushrooms in butter 5 minutes. Stir in flour, 1 teaspoon salt and the pepper. Cook over low heat, stirring until mixture is bubbly. Remove from heat and stir in half-and-half. Heat to boiling, stirring constantly. Remove from heat. Gradually stir part of the hot mixture into egg yolk, then blend into the hot mixture in the saucepan. Stir in olives and crabmeat.

Spoon the crabmeat mixture into the avocado halves and sprinkle with cheese. Bake 20 minutes or until heated through.

4 SERVINGS.

VARIATION

Tuna Avocado: Substitute 2 cans (6½ ounces each) tuna, drained, for the crabmeat.

SALMON ROMANOFF

8 ounces uncooked medium noodles
1½ cups creamed cottage cheese
1 to 1½ cups dairy sour cream
½ cup finely chopped onion
1 clove garlic, minced
1 to 2 teaspoons Worcestershire sauce
Dash of cayenne red pepper
½ teaspoon salt
1 can (16 ounces) salmon, drained
½ cup shredded sharp cheese

Heat oven to 325°. Cook the noodles as directed on package; drain. Mix noodles and the remaining ingredients except the sharp cheese.

Pour into a greased 2-quart casserole. Sprinkle with cheese. Bake uncovered 40 minutes. Garnish with parsley and lemon wedges.

6 TO 8 SERVINGS.

AVERY ISLAND DEVILED SHRIMP

Deviled Shrimp Sauce (below)
1 egg, slightly beaten
¼ teaspoon salt
2 cups cleaned cooked shrimp*
½ cup dry bread crumbs
¼ cup butter or margarine
2 cups hot cooked rice

*From 1½ pounds fresh or frozen raw shrimp (in shells), 2 packages (6 ounces each) frozen peeled shrimp or 2 cans (4½ or 5 ounces each) shrimp.

Prepare Deviled Shrimp Sauce. Mix egg and salt. Dip shrimp in egg, then coat with bread crumbs. Melt butter in a skillet and brown shrimp over medium heat. Serve shrimp on rice and pour hot sauce over shrimp.

4 SERVINGS.

DEVILED SHRIMP SAUCE

1 medium onion, chopped
1 clove garlic, minced
2 tablespoons butter or margarine
1 can (10¾ ounces) condensed chicken broth
½ cup water
2 tablespoons steak sauce
1½ teaspoons dry mustard
½ teaspoon salt
¼ to ½ teaspoon red pepper sauce
1 to 2 tablespoons lemon juice

Cook and stir onion and garlic in butter until onion is tender. Stir in remaining ingredients except lemon juice. Heat to boiling, stirring occasionally, then simmer 15 minutes. Stir in lemon juice.

½ **cup water**
¼ **cup butter or margarine**
½ **cup all-purpose flour***
⅛ **teaspoon salt**
½ **to 1 teaspoon caraway seed**
2 **eggs**
  Tuna Salad (below)

*If using self-rising flour, omit salt.

This giant cream puff shell makes a spectacular showcase dessert (without the caraway seed, of course). Fill it with a mixture of sweetened whipped cream and strawberries or with scoops of ice cream, sundaed with a sauce. Very impressive!

The salads, too, can solo superbly. All they need is a bed of crisp greens.

TUNA SALAD IN CARAWAY PUFF BOWL

Heat oven to 400°. Grease a 9-inch glass pie plate. Heat water and butter to a rolling boil in a medium saucepan. Quickly stir in flour, salt and caraway seed. Stir vigorously over low heat until the mixture forms a ball, about 1 minute. Remove from heat.

Beat in eggs, all at one time, and continue beating until smooth. Spread the batter evenly in the pie plate. (Have batter touching the side of the plate, but do not spread it up the side.) Bake 45 to 50 minutes or until puffed and golden brown.

Just before serving, mound the Tuna Salad in the puff bowl. Garnish with parsley, sliced tomatoes or hard-cooked eggs. To serve, cut into wedges.

8 SERVINGS.

TUNA SALAD
2 **cans (6½ ounces each) tuna, drained**
1 **cup cut-up celery**
½ **cup cubed avocado or ½ cup chopped green or ripe olives**
¼ **cup chopped onion**
1 **tablespoon lemon juice**
3 **hard-cooked eggs, cut up**
½ **teaspoon curry powder, if desired**
¾ **to 1 cup mayonnaise**

Combine all ingredients except the mayonnaise. Cover and chill. Just before serving, fold mayonnaise into the tuna mixture.

VARIATIONS

Chicken Salad: Substitute 2 cups cut-up cooked chicken for the tuna.

Shrimp Salad: Substitute 2 cans (4½ ounces each) shrimp, rinsed and drained, for the tuna.

Salads and Vegetables

FRENCH DRESSING

1 cup olive oil or salad oil
¼ cup vinegar
¼ cup lemon juice
1 teaspoon salt
½ teaspoon dry mustard
½ teaspoon paprika

Shake all ingredients in a tightly covered jar; refrigerate. Shake again just before serving.

1½ CUPS.

SWEET GARLIC DRESSING

¼ cup sugar
½ teaspoon salt
1 clove garlic, crushed
  Dash of pepper
2 to 3 tablespoons olive oil
  or salad oil
¼ cup vinegar

Shake all ingredients in a tightly covered jar. Refrigerate several hours to blend flavors. Shake again just before serving. This sweet oil and vinegar dressing is especially good with sliced tomatoes, a slaw or a tossed green salad.

ABOUT ½ CUP.

BLUE CHEESE DRESSING

1 cup dairy sour cream
2 green onions, finely chopped
2 tablespoons mayonnaise
2 tablespoons lemon juice
½ cup crumbled blue cheese
  Salt and pepper to taste

Mix all ingredients in a small bowl. Cover and refrigerate at least 2 hours to blend flavors. A perfect accent for any salad of greens or vegetables.

ABOUT 1½ CUPS.

COOKED SALAD DRESSING

¼ cup all-purpose flour
2 tablespoons sugar
1 teaspoon salt
1 teaspoon dry mustard
2 egg yolks
1½ cups milk
⅓ cup vinegar
1 tablespoon butter or margarine

Mix flour, sugar, salt and mustard in a medium saucepan. Beat egg yolks slightly and stir in milk. Stir the egg-milk mixture into the flour mixture.

Cook over medium heat, stirring constantly, until the mixture thickens and boils. Boil and stir 1 minute. Remove from heat and stir in vinegar and butter. Cool thoroughly. Try mixing with an equal amount of dairy sour cream or whipped cream.

ABOUT 2 CUPS.

Pictured on the preceding page:
Old-fashioned Potato Salad,
Chive-buttered Carrots,
Tomatoes Vinaigrette

GOURMET TOSSED GREEN SALAD

1 large head lettuce, washed and chilled
¼ pound fresh mushrooms, sliced (about 2 cups)
1 small cauliflower, separated into tiny flowerets (about 2½ cups)
1 small Bermuda onion, sliced thinly and separated into rings
1 medium green pepper, diced (about ⅔ cup)
½ cup sliced pimiento-stuffed green olives
½ cup crumbled blue cheese
Classic French Dressing (right)

Tear the lettuce into bite-size pieces (about 10 cups). Add remaining ingredients except Classic French Dressing and toss. Cover and chill thoroughly, at least 1 hour. Just before serving, toss with the dressing.

8 TO 10 SERVINGS.

CLASSIC FRENCH DRESSING

¼ cup olive oil, salad oil or combination
2 tablespoons wine or tarragon vinegar
1 small clove garlic, crushed
¾ teaspoon salt
Generous dash of freshly ground pepper

Just before serving, toss the salad with oil until the greens glisten. Mix vinegar and seasonings thoroughly. Pour over the salad and toss.

TOSSED ARTICHOKE AND OLIVE SALAD

8 ounces spinach
1 large head lettuce, washed and chilled
2 jars (6 ounces each) marinated artichoke hearts
2 cans (3⅞ ounces each) pitted ripe olives, drained
French Dressing (page 32) or bottled herb salad dressing

Wash spinach; remove the stems and dry the leaves. Tear the spinach leaves and lettuce into bite-size pieces (about 12 cups). For an easy tossing trick, divide the greens evenly between 2 large plastic bags and refrigerate.

Just before serving, add 1 jar artichoke hearts (with the liquid), 1 can olives and ⅓ cup salad dressing to each bag. Close the bags tightly and shake until the greens are well coated with dressing.

12 SERVINGS.

10 to 12 ounces fresh spinach
1 clove garlic, peeled and slivered
⅓ cup salad oil
¼ cup red wine vinegar
¼ teaspoon salt
    Dash of pepper
2 hard-cooked eggs, chopped
3 slices bacon, crisply fried and crumbled

HOT SPINACH SALAD

Wash spinach; remove the stems and dry the leaves. Tear into bite-size pieces (about 10 cups) and refrigerate. Let garlic stand in oil 1 hour, then remove garlic.

Just before serving, heat oil, vinegar, salt and pepper in a chafing dish or small saucepan, stirring occasionally. Toss the hot dressing with the spinach until leaves are well coated. Sprinkle eggs and bacon over the salad and toss lightly.

4 TO 6 SERVINGS.

2 bunches leaf lettuce, washed and chilled
½ cup half-and-half
1 to 1½ tablespoons sugar
¼ teaspoon salt
3 to 4 tablespoons vinegar

GRANDMOTHER'S LETTUCE SALAD

Tear the leaf lettuce into bite-size pieces (about 6 cups). Just before serving, mix half-and-half, sugar, salt and vinegar. Pour over lettuce and toss.

5 OR 6 SERVINGS.

2 cups finely shredded carrots (3 to 4 medium)
⅓ cup raisins
1 tablespoon snipped chives
¼ teaspoon salt
    Cooked Salad Dressing (page 32) or mayonnaise

CARROT-RAISIN SALAD

Combine carrots, raisins, chives and salt in a bowl. Add just enough salad dressing to moisten the ingredients and toss lightly. We like to serve this salad in lettuce cups and garnished with parsley.

4 OR 5 SERVINGS.

Note: Use your blender to chop the carrots. Cut them into ½-inch slices. Place half the carrot slices in blender and add water just to cover carrots.

Cover and follow manufacturer's instructions or run just long enough to finely chop carrots (3 to 5 seconds). Empty carrots into a strainer and drain thoroughly. Repeat with the remaining carrots.

CABBAGE-RED APPLE SALAD

5 cups shredded or finely
   chopped cabbage (about
   1 small head)
1 unpared red apple, diced
½ cup sliced celery
1 teaspoon salt
   Mayonnaise or Cooked Salad
   Dressing (page 32)

Combine cabbage, apple, celery and salt in a bowl. Add just enough mayonnaise to moisten and toss. Chill before serving.

6 TO 8 SERVINGS.

VARIATION

Cabbage-Pineapple Salad: Add 1 can (8¼ ounces) crushed pineapple, drained, and ½ cup miniature marshmallows.

OLD-FASHIONED CABBAGE SLAW

1 teaspoon salt
¼ teaspoon pepper
½ teaspoon dry mustard
½ teaspoon celery seed
2 tablespoons sugar
¼ cup chopped green pepper
1 tablespoon chopped pimiento
1 teaspoon instant minced onion
3 tablespoons salad oil
⅓ cup white vinegar
4 cups finely shredded or chopped
   cabbage (about ½ medium head)

Combine all the ingredients in a large bowl. Cover and chill thoroughly, at least 3 hours.

Just before serving, drain the cabbage. Garnish with watercress and sliced pimiento-stuffed olives.

6 SERVINGS.

KIDNEY BEAN SALAD

1 can (20 ounces) kidney beans,
   drained
¼ cup diced celery
3 dill or sweet pickles, chopped
1 small onion, minced
½ teaspoon salt
⅛ teaspoon pepper
   About ¼ cup mayonnaise or
   dairy sour cream
2 hard-cooked eggs, sliced

Mix all ingredients except the eggs. Add eggs and toss lightly. Chill thoroughly, at least 4 hours. Serve the salad on a bed of crisp greens and garnish with grated cheese or onion rings.

6 SERVINGS.

24-Hour Salad

CUCUMBER RELISH MOLD

1 package (3 ounces) lime-flavored
    gelatin
1 cup drained shredded pared
    cucumber
1 cup thinly sliced celery
3 tablespoons thinly sliced
    green onions
½ teaspoon salt
    Mayonnaise

Prepare gelatin as directed on package except — decrease the water to 1½ cups. Chill until slightly thickened but not set. Fold in the vegetables and salt. Pour into a 4-cup mold or 4 to 6 individual molds. Chill until firm. Unmold onto a lettuce-lined plate and serve with mayonnaise.

4 TO 6 SERVINGS.

24-HOUR SALAD

Old-fashioned Fruit Dressing
    (below)
1 can (17 ounces) pitted light
    or dark sweet cherries, drained
2 cans (15½ ounces each)
    pineapple chunks, drained and
    cut in half (reserve 2 tablespoons
    syrup for the dressing)
3 oranges, pared, sectioned and
    cut up, or 2 cans (11 ounces
    each) mandarin orange
    segments, drained
1 cup miniature marshmallows

Prepare Old-fashioned Fruit Dressing. Combine fruits and marshmallows. Pour the dressing over the ingredients and toss. Cover and chill 12 to 24 hours.

Serve in a salad bowl or in lettuce cups. If you like, garnish with orange sections and maraschino cherries.

8 TO 10 SERVINGS.

OLD-FASHIONED FRUIT DRESSING

2 eggs, beaten
2 tablespoons sugar
2 tablespoons vinegar or lemon juice
2 tablespoons pineapple syrup (from
    the canned pineapple chunks)
1 tablespoon butter or margarine
    Dash of salt
¾ cup chilled whipping cream

Combine all ingredients except the whipping cream in a small saucepan. Heat just to boiling, stirring constantly. Remove from heat and cool. In a chilled bowl, beat the cream until stiff. Fold in the egg mixture.

TOMATOES VINAIGRETTE

8 to 12 thick slices tomato or
   peeled small tomatoes
1 cup olive oil or salad oil
⅓ cup wine vinegar
2 teaspoons oregano leaves
1 teaspoon salt
½ teaspoon pepper
½ teaspoon dry mustard
2 cloves garlic, crushed
   Crisp lettuce leaves
   Minced green onion
   Snipped parsley

If using small tomatoes, cut off the stem ends. Arrange tomatoes in a baking dish, 8 x 8 x 2 inches. Shake oil, vinegar, oregano, salt, pepper, mustard and garlic in a tightly covered jar. Pour over the tomatoes. Cover and chill at least 2 hours, spooning the dressing over the tomatoes from time to time.

Just before serving, arrange tomatoes on lettuce leaves. Sprinkle tomatoes with onion and parsley and drizzle some of the dressing on top.

5 TO 8 SERVINGS.

CRANBERRY RELISH SALAD

4 cups cranberries
1½ cups sugar
1 cup chilled whipping cream
2 cups Tokay grapes, halved
   and seeded
1 can (15½ ounces) crushed
   pineapple, drained
½ cup coarsely chopped walnuts
   or pecans

Finely chop cranberries. Sprinkle sugar over cranberries and let stand 1 hour.

Drain cranberries thoroughly. In a chilled bowl, beat whipping cream until stiff. Combine grapes, pineapple, nuts and cranberries; fold in the whipped cream. Serve the salad in lettuce cups.

This triple-treat recipe can serve as a side-salad, as an accompaniment for poultry and as a dessert.

6 TO 8 SERVINGS.

Note: 1 package (10 ounces) frozen cranberry relish, thawed and drained, can be substituted for the cranberries and sugar.

OLD-FASHIONED POTATO SALAD

2 pounds potatoes (about 6 medium)
¼ cup French Dressing (page 32) or bottled French or Italian dressing
1 cup sliced celery
1 cup cubed cucumber
¾ cup minced onion
½ cup thinly sliced radishes
½ cup Cooked Salad Dressing (page 32) or mayonnaise
½ cup dairy sour cream
1 tablespoon prepared mustard
2 teaspoons lemon juice
1½ teaspoons salt
¼ teaspoon pepper
4 hard-cooked eggs, chopped

Cook the unpared potatoes until tender, 30 to 35 minutes. Drain and cool slightly. Peel the potatoes and cut into cubes.

Pour French Dressing over warm potatoes in a large bowl and toss. Cover and refrigerate at least 4 hours.

Add celery, cucumber, onion and radishes to the potatoes. Mix Cooked Salad Dressing, sour cream, mustard, lemon juice, salt and pepper; pour over the salad and toss. Carefully stir in chopped eggs. Chill. Serve the salad in a bowl lined with crisp lettuce leaves; for color, garnish with parsley, sliced tomatoes or hard-cooked eggs.

6 SERVINGS.

HOT GERMAN POTATO SALAD

3 pounds potatoes (about 9 medium)
6 slices bacon
¾ cup chopped onion
2 tablespoons flour
2 tablespoons sugar
2 teaspoons salt
½ teaspoon celery seed
Dash of pepper
¾ cup water
⅓ cup vinegar

Pare the potatoes and cook until tender, 30 to 35 minutes. Drain and set aside.

In a large skillet, fry bacon until crisp; remove and drain. Cook and stir chopped onion in bacon drippings until tender and golden. Stir in flour, sugar, salt, celery seed and pepper. Cook over low heat, stirring until bubbly. Remove from heat and stir in water and vinegar. Heat to boiling, stirring constantly. Boil and stir 1 minute. Remove the skillet from heat.

Crumble the bacon and slice the potatoes. Carefully stir bacon and potatoes into the hot mixture in the skillet. Heat through, stirring lightly to coat potato slices.

5 OR 6 SERVINGS.

SKILLET-CREAMED POTATOES

6 pared medium potatoes,
cooked and drained, or 2 cans
(16 ounces each) whole potatoes
2 cups dairy sour cream
¼ cup finely chopped onion
2 tablespoons finely chopped
pimiento-stuffed olives
1 teaspoon salt
½ teaspoon pepper
Paprika
Snipped parsley
Pimiento-stuffed olives, sliced

Cut potatoes into ½-inch cubes. Combine sour cream, onion, chopped olives, salt and pepper in a large skillet. Add potatoes; heat over medium heat, stirring frequently, until the cream bubbles and potatoes are heated through. Garnish with the paprika, parsley and sliced olives.

6 SERVINGS.

TWICE-BAKED POTATOES

4 large baking potatoes
Shortening
⅓ to ½ cup milk
¼ cup soft butter or margarine
½ teaspoon salt
Dash of pepper
4 tablespoons finely shredded
cheese

Heat oven to 375°. Scrub the potatoes; rub them with shortening and prick with a fork. Bake until potatoes are tender, 1 to 1¼ hours.

Increase oven temperature to 400°. Cut a thin slice from the top of each potato and scoop out the inside, leaving a thin shell. Mash potatoes until no lumps remain. Add milk in small amounts, beating after each addition. (The amount of milk needed to make potatoes smooth and fluffy depends on the kind of potatoes used.) Add butter, salt and pepper. Beat until potatoes are light and fluffy.

Fill potato shells with mashed potatoes and sprinkle each with 1 tablespoon shredded cheese. Bake 20 minutes or until golden.

4 SERVINGS.

VARIATION

Pepper or Pimiento Potatoes: Stir ¼ cup finely chopped green pepper or ¼ cup drained chopped pimiento into the mashed potato mixture.

BUFFET POTATOES

2 pounds potatoes
  (about 6 medium)
  Pepper
1 teaspoon salt
3 tablespoons snipped parsley
¼ cup chopped onion
¾ cup shredded sharp process
  cheese
3 tablespoons butter or margarine
¾ cup half-and-half

Heat oven to 350°. Pare the potatoes and cut into lengthwise strips, ¼ to ⅜ inch wide.

Arrange potatoes in a greased 2-quart casserole in 3 layers, topping each layer with a dash of pepper and ⅓ each of the salt, parsley, onion and cheese. Dot with butter and pour half-and-half over potatoes. Cover and bake 1 hour. Uncover and bake 30 minutes longer or until potatoes are tender.

6 TO 8 SERVINGS.

SWEET POTATO-APPLESAUCE BAKE

1 pound sweet potatoes or yams
  (about 3 medium) or 1 can
  (18 ounces) vacuum-pack sweet
  potatoes
½ teaspoon salt
1 can (8 ounces) applesauce
⅓ cup brown sugar (packed)
¼ cup chopped nuts
½ teaspoon cinnamon
2 tablespoons butter or margarine

If using fresh sweet potatoes or yams, cook unpared potatoes until tender, 30 to 35 minutes. Drain and cool slightly. Slip off skins.

Heat oven to 375°. Cut each sweet potato lengthwise in half. Place halves in an ungreased baking dish, 8 x 8 x 2 inches. Sprinkle with salt and spread applesauce on potatoes. Mix sugar, nuts and cinnamon and sprinkle over the applesauce. Dot with butter and cover with aluminum foil. Bake 30 minutes or until hot and bubbly.

4 TO 6 SERVINGS.

GOURMET GOLDEN SQUASH

3 pounds Hubbard squash, pared
  and cubed (about 6 cups)
2 tablespoons butter or margarine
1 cup dairy sour cream
½ cup finely chopped onion
1 teaspoon salt
¼ teaspoon pepper

Cook squash until tender, 15 to 20 minutes; drain. Heat oven to 400°. Mash squash and stir in the remaining ingredients. Mound the mixture in an ungreased 1-quart casserole. Bake uncovered 20 minutes or until heated through.

6 TO 8 SERVINGS.

HARVARD BEETS

5 medium beets (about 1¼ pounds)
1 tablespoon cornstarch
1 tablespoon sugar
¾ teaspoon salt
   Dash of pepper
⅔ cup water
¼ cup vinegar

Cook beets until tender, 35 to 45 minutes. Drain and cool slightly. Slip off skins and cut into slices.

Mix cornstarch, sugar, salt and pepper in a small saucepan. Gradually stir in water and vinegar. Cook, stirring constantly, until the mixture thickens and boils. Boil and stir 1 minute. Stir in the beets and heat through.

4 SERVINGS.

CHIVE-BUTTERED CARROTS

1½ pounds carrots or 2 cans
    (16 ounces each) whole carrots,
    drained
¼ cup butter or margarine
¼ teaspoon seasoned salt
⅛ teaspoon pepper
1 tablespoon snipped chives
   or minced onion

If using fresh carrots, cook until tender, 20 to 25 minutes; drain.

Melt butter in a large skillet and add carrots. Sprinkle with salt, pepper and chives. Heat through, turning carrots occasionally to coat with butter.

5 OR 6 SERVINGS.

GOLDEN CORN PUDDING

1 can (16 ounces) whole kernel
   corn, drained (about 2 cups)
1 teaspoon sugar
1 teaspoon salt
⅛ teaspoon pepper
2 eggs, well beaten
1 cup milk
1 tablespoon butter or margarine,
   melted
2 tablespoons cracker crumbs
2 tablespoons chopped green
   pepper
1 teaspoon chopped pimiento

Heat oven to 350°. Mix all ingredients thoroughly and pour into a greased 1-quart casserole. Place the casserole in a baking pan. Pour very hot water into the pan — to a depth of about 1 inch. Bake 50 to 60 minutes or until a knife inserted 1 inch from the edge of the casserole comes out clean. (The center will be soft but will set.)

6 SERVINGS.

DELUXE CREAMED ONIONS

2 pounds small white onions
or 2 cans (16 ounces each)
whole onions
2 tablespoons butter or margarine
2 tablespoons flour
½ teaspoon salt
⅛ teaspoon pepper
1½ cups half-and-half
1½ cups shredded carrots

If using fresh onions, peel and cook until tender, 15 to 20 minutes; drain. If using canned onions, simply heat and drain.

Melt butter in a large saucepan over low heat. Blend in flour and seasonings. Cook over low heat, stirring until the mixture is smooth and bubbly. Immediately stir in half-and-half. Heat to boiling, stirring constantly. Boil and stir 1 minute. Stir in carrots and cook about 5 minutes longer. Pour the sauce over the hot onions.

6 SERVINGS.

CLOVED ONIONS

1½ pounds small white onions
or 1 can (16 ounces) whole
onions, drained
3 tablespoons butter or margarine
⅛ teaspoon ground cloves
⅓ cup brown sugar (packed)

If using fresh onions, peel and cook until tender, 15 to 20 minutes; drain.

Melt butter with cloves in a large skillet over medium heat, stirring occasionally. Add onions and stir gently until coated. Sprinkle brown sugar over onions; cook, turning frequently, about 5 minutes — until onions are golden and glazed.

4 SERVINGS.

SPINACH GOURMET

1 pound fresh spinach or 1
package (10 ounces) frozen
chopped spinach
1 jar (4½ ounces) button
mushrooms, drained
1 teaspoon instant minced onion
1 small clove garlic, crushed
½ teaspoon salt
Dash of pepper
⅓ cup dairy sour cream
1 tablespoon half-and-half
or milk

Cook spinach until tender, 3 to 5 minutes; drain. Combine spinach, mushrooms and seasonings in a saucepan. Blend sour cream and half-and-half. Pour over the spinach mixture and heat just to boiling.

4 SERVINGS.

FRENCH FRIED ONION RINGS

1   **large Spanish or Bermuda onion**
⅔   **cup milk**
½   **cup all-purpose flour***
¾   **teaspoon baking powder**
¼   **teaspoon salt**

*If using self-rising flour, omit baking powder and salt.

Cut the onion into ¼-inch slices and separate into rings. In a large skillet, heat fat or oil (1 inch deep) to 375°. (The fat is hot enough if a 1-inch cube of bread browns in 60 seconds.) Beat the remaining ingredients until smooth.

Dip onion rings into the batter and let the excess batter drip back into the bowl. Fry a few onion rings at a time until golden brown, about 2 minutes. Turn only once. Drain. Serve hot.

3 OR 4 SERVINGS.

Note: To keep warm, place in 300° oven until ready to serve. Or make them several hours ahead of time and heat 7 to 10 minutes.

ZUCCHINI PROVENÇALE

4   **small zucchini (about 1 pound)**
1   **onion, thinly sliced**
½   **cup finely chopped green pepper**
2   **tablespoons salad oil**
1   **clove garlic, crushed**
1   **teaspoon salt**
⅛   **teaspoon pepper**
2   **tomatoes, peeled and cut into wedges**
    Snipped parsley
    Grated Parmesan cheese

Cut the unpared zucchini into ¼-inch slices (about 2 cups). Cook and stir all ingredients except the tomato wedges, parsley and cheese in a medium skillet until heated through. Cover and cook over medium heat, stirring occasionally, until the vegetables are crisp-tender, about 5 minutes.

Add tomato wedges. Cover and cook over low heat just until tomatoes are heated through, about 3 minutes. Sprinkle with parsley and cheese.

4 SERVINGS.

Breads

2 packages active dry yeast
½ cup warm water (105 to 115°)
1½ cups lukewarm milk (scalded
    then cooled)
¼ cup sugar
1 tablespoon salt
3 eggs
¼ cup shortening or butter or
    margarine, softened
7¼ to 7½ cups all-purpose flour*
2 cups raisins

*If using self-rising flour, omit salt.

A tender, rich, yellow-yummy bread — thanks to the eggs — that makes just about the best toast ever. A "rather not" on the raisins? Forget about them. You'll find you've made our equally well-known Rich Egg Bread.

Pictured on the preceding page:
Cinnamon Whirligig,
Pumpernickel Bread,
Pumpkin Bread,
French Breakfast Puffs

NEW ENGLAND RAISIN BREAD

Dissolve yeast in warm water. Stir in milk, sugar, salt, eggs, shortening and about 3½ cups of the flour. Beat until smooth. Mix in raisins and enough of the remaining flour to make the dough easy to handle.

Turn the dough onto a lightly floured board and knead until smooth and elastic, about 5 minutes. Place in a greased bowl; turn the greased side up. Cover and let rise in a warm place until double, 1½ to 2 hours.

Punch down the dough and divide in half. Roll each half into a rectangle, 18 x 9 inches. Roll up, beginning at the short side. With the side of your hand, press down on each end to seal; fold under loaf. Place seam side down in a greased loaf pan, 9 x 5 x 3 or 8½ x 4½ x 2½ inches. Let rise until double, about 1 hour.

Heat oven to 400°. Bake on low rack 25 to 30 minutes or until the loaves are golden brown and sound hollow when tapped. Immediately remove from the pans and cool. Brush with butter or shortening or frost with Creamy Icing (page 58).

2 LOAVES.

VARIATION

Rich Egg Braid: Omit raisins. After punching down dough, divide into thirds. Divide each third into 3 equal parts; shape each into a strand, about 14 inches long. Loosely braid each group of 3 strands on a greased baking sheet. Pinch ends and tuck under. Brush with butter. Cover and let rise until double, 40 to 50 minutes. Mix 1 egg yolk and 2 tablespoons cold water; brush on braid. Heat oven to 375°. Bake 25 to 30 minutes. 3 BRAIDS.

BUTTERMILK HERB BREAD

2 packages active dry yeast
¾ cup warm water (105 to 115°)
2 teaspoons caraway seed
½ teaspoon crumbled leaf sage
½ teaspoon nutmeg
1¼ cups buttermilk
4½ to 5 cups all-purpose flour*
¼ cup shortening
2 tablespoons sugar
2 teaspoons baking powder
2 teaspoons salt
   Soft butter or margarine

*If using self-rising flour, omit baking powder and salt.

A timesaving yeast bread? This one was developed especially for the electric mixer. And it requires only one rising! So why not make two of these "can-do-quick" loaves while you're at it. Just double all ingredients except the yeast. Blend 1 minute on low speed, scraping the bowl constantly. Beat 4 minutes on medium speed, scraping occasionally. Then stir in the remaining flour. Knead, divide the dough in half and shape into two loaves.

Grease a loaf pan, 9 x 5 x 3 inches. Dissolve yeast in warm water in a large mixer bowl. Stir in caraway seed, sage and nutmeg. Add buttermilk, 2½ cups of the flour, the shortening, sugar, baking powder and salt. Blend ½ minute on low speed, scraping the bowl constantly. Beat 2 minutes on medium speed, scraping occasionally. Stir in the remaining flour. (The dough should remain soft and slightly sticky.)

Turn the dough onto a well-floured board and knead until smooth, about 5 minutes. Roll the dough into a rectangle, 18 x 9 inches. Roll up, beginning at the short side. With the side of your hand, press down on each end to seal; fold under loaf. Place seam side down in the pan. Brush the loaf lightly with butter. Let rise in a warm place until double, about 1 hour. (The dough in the center should be about 2 inches above the pan.)

Heat oven to 425°. Place the oven rack in the lowest position or bread will brown too quickly. Bake 30 to 35 minutes. (If the loaf is browning too quickly, cover with foil for the last 15 minutes of baking.) Immediately remove from the pan and cool on a wire rack. For a soft, shiny crust, brush the top with butter or shortening.

VARIATIONS

Garlic Bread: Omit caraway seed, leaf sage and nutmeg and add ¾ teaspoon garlic powder.

Whole Wheat Bread: Omit caraway seed, leaf sage and nutmeg. Substitute 1½ cups all-purpose flour and 1 cup whole wheat flour for the first addition of flour; substitute 2 cups whole wheat flour for the second addition of flour.

¾ **cup boiling water**
½ **cup oats**
3 **tablespoons shortening**
¼ **cup light molasses**
2 **teaspoons salt**
1 **package active dry yeast**
¼ **cup warm water (105 to 115°)**
1 **egg**
2¾ **cups all-purpose flour***

*If using self-rising flour, omit salt.

Batter breads like these are shortcut yeast breads. They require no kneading or shaping so they're easier to make and take about half the time. You simply mix the ingredients with an electric mixer and spread the batter evenly in the pan. (Batter breads have a more open texture than kneaded breads, but they're very moist and tender.)

A word of caution: Too much rising will cause the loaf to collapse. If the dough should rise too high in the pan, simply remove it, punch it down and let it rise again.

EASY OATMEAL BREAD

Grease a loaf pan, 9 x 5 x 3 or 8½ x 4½ x 2½ inches. Combine boiling water, oats, shortening, molasses and salt in a large mixer bowl. Cool to lukewarm.

Dissolve yeast in warm water. Add yeast, egg and 1½ cups of the flour to the oat mixture. Beat 2 minutes on medium speed, scraping the bowl frequently. Stir in the remaining flour until smooth.

Spread the batter evenly in the pan. The batter will be sticky — smooth and pat into shape with floured hands. Let rise in a warm place until the batter is 1 inch from the top of the 9-inch pan or reaches the top of the 8½-inch pan, about 1½ hours.

Heat oven to 375°. Bake 50 to 55 minutes or until the loaf is brown and sounds hollow when tapped. (If the loaf is browning too quickly, cover with foil for the last 15 minutes of baking.) Remove from the pan and cool on a wire rack. For a soft, shiny crust, brush the top with butter or shortening.

VARIATIONS

Anadama Batter Bread: Substitute ½ cup yellow cornmeal for the oats.

Little Loaves: Grease 6 miniature loaf pans, 4½ x 2½ x 1½ inches. Divide the batter among the pans and let rise until it just reaches the tops of the pans, about 1½ hours. Bake 35 to 40 minutes.

SWEDISH LIMPA RYE BREAD

2 packages active dry yeast
1½ cups warm water (105 to 115°)
¼ cup molasses
⅓ cup sugar
1 tablespoon salt
2 tablespoons shortening
    Grated peel of 1 to 2 oranges
2½ cups medium rye flour
2¼ to 2¾ cups all-purpose flour*
    Cornmeal

*If using self-rising flour, omit salt.

Dissolve yeast in warm water. Stir in molasses, sugar, salt, shortening, orange peel and rye flour. Beat until smooth. Mix in enough of the white flour to make the dough easy to handle.

Turn the dough onto a lightly floured board. Cover and let rest 10 to 15 minutes. Knead until smooth, about 5 minutes. Place in a greased bowl; turn the greased side up. Cover and let rise in a warm place until double, about 1 hour. (The dough is ready if an indentation remains when touched.)

Punch down the dough; round up, cover and let rise until double, about 40 minutes.

Grease a baking sheet and sprinkle with cornmeal. Punch down the dough and divide in half. Shape each half into a slightly flattened round loaf. Place the loaves in opposite corners of the baking sheet. Cover and let rise 1 hour.

Heat oven to 375°. Bake 30 to 35 minutes. Cool on a wire rack.

2 LOAVES.

PUMPERNICKEL BREAD

3 packages active dry yeast
1½ cups warm water (105 to 115°)
½ cup molasses
3 teaspoons salt
2 tablespoons shortening
2 tablespoons caraway seed
2¾ cups rye flour
2¼ to 2¾ cups all-purpose flour*
    Cornmeal

*If using self-rising flour, omit salt.

Dissolve yeast in warm water. Stir in molasses, salt, shortening, caraway seed and rye flour. Beat until smooth. Mix in enough of the white flour to make the dough easy to handle.

Knead and shape as directed for Swedish Limpa Rye Bread (above). Bake 25 to 30 minutes.

2 LOAVES.

1 **package active dry yeast**
1½ **cups warm water (105 to 115°)**
⅔ **cup sugar**
1½ **teaspoons salt**
⅔ **cup shortening**
2 **eggs**
1 **cup lukewarm mashed potatoes**
6½ **to 7 cups all-purpose flour***
   Soft butter or margarine

*If using self-rising flour, omit salt.

POTATO REFRIGERATOR ROLLS

Dissolve yeast in warm water. Stir in sugar, salt, shortening, eggs, potatoes and 4 cups of the flour. Beat until smooth. Mix in enough of the remaining flour to make the dough easy to handle.

Turn the dough onto a lightly floured board and knead until smooth and elastic, about 5 minutes. Place in a greased bowl; turn the greased side up. Cover bowl tightly and refrigerate until ready to use. (The dough can be refrigerated at 45° or below for up to 5 days. Keep covered.) If the dough rises, punch it down occasionally.

When you want to make fresh rolls, punch down the dough and cut off the amount needed. Use ¼ of the dough for each of the shapes below. Shape, cover and let rise in a warm place until double, 45 to 60 minutes.

Heat oven to 400°. Bake rolls 13 to 15 minutes.

Cloverleaf: Shape bits of dough into 1-inch balls. Place 3 balls in each greased medium muffin cup. Brush with butter. ABOUT 12 ROLLS.

Cobblestone: Shape bits of dough into 1½-inch balls. Place in a lightly greased layer pan, 9 x 1½ inches. Brush with butter. 2 DOZEN ROLLS.

Four-leaf Clover: Shape pieces of dough into 2-inch balls. Place each ball in a greased medium muffin cup. With scissors, snip each ball in half, then into quarters. Brush with butter. ABOUT 12 ROLLS.

Parker House: Roll dough into a rectangle, 13 x 9 inches, and cut into 3-inch circles. Brush with butter. Fold so the top half overlaps slightly. Press the edges together. Place on a lightly greased baking sheet. Brush with butter. ABOUT 10 ROLLS.

You can't beat the fragrance and flavor of homemade rolls. And with this do-ahead, keep-on-hand dough, you can boast hot-from-the-oven rolls on even your busiest days.

1. For quick Four-leaf Clovers, just snip each ball in half and then in half again.
2. For Parker House rolls, fold the circles slightly off-center to make sure the top half overlaps.

BRAN PAN BISCUITS

1 package active dry yeast
1 cup warm water (105 to 115°)
¼ cup brown sugar (packed)
1½ teaspoons salt
½ cup whole bran or oats
1 egg
3 tablespoons shortening
3½ to 3¾ cups all-purpose flour*

*If using self-rising flour, omit salt.

Dissolve yeast in warm water. Stir in sugar, salt, bran, egg, shortening and 1¾ cups of the flour. Beat until smooth. Mix in enough of the remaining flour to make the dough easy to handle.

Place the dough in a greased bowl; turn the greased side up. Cover and let rise in a warm place until double, about 1½ hours. (The dough is ready if an indentation remains when touched.)

Punch down the dough and, with greased hands, shape into 1½-inch balls. (The dough will be slightly sticky.) Place in 2 greased layer pans, 9 x 1½ inches. Cover and let rise until double, about 45 minutes.

Heat oven to 375°. Bake 20 to 25 minutes.

2 DOZEN BISCUITS.

DILL BATTER BUNS

¾ cup dairy sour cream
1 package active dry yeast
¼ cup warm water (105 to 115°)
2 tablespoons sugar
1 teaspoon salt
2 tablespoons shortening
1 egg
1½ tablespoons fresh dill seed or snipped chives
2¼ cups all-purpose flour*

*If using self-rising flour, omit salt.

Heat sour cream *just* to lukewarm. Dissolve yeast in warm water. Stir in sour cream, sugar, salt, shortening, egg, dill seed and about 1½ cups of the flour. Beat until smooth. Stir in the remaining flour until smooth. Cover and let rise in a warm place until double, about 30 minutes.

Grease 16 medium muffin cups. Stir down the batter and fill the cups ½ full. (The batter will be sticky — smooth and pat into shape with floured fingers.) Let rise until the dough reaches the tops of the muffin cups, 20 to 30 minutes.

Heat oven to 400°. Bake 15 to 20 minutes or until golden brown.

16 BUNS.

QUICK CORN BREAD

1¼ cups buttermilk baking mix
¾ cup cornmeal
2 tablespoons sugar
½ teaspoon salt
1 egg
2 tablespoons shortening
⅔ cup milk

Heat oven to 400°. Grease a baking pan, 8 x 8 x 2 inches. Mix all ingredients with a spoon and beat vigorously ½ minute. Spread in the pan. Bake 20 to 25 minutes. Serve warm.

8 SERVINGS.

POPOVERS

2 eggs
1 cup milk
1 cup all-purpose flour*
½ teaspoon salt

*Do not use self-rising flour in this recipe.

Heat oven to 450°. Grease 6 deep custard cups or 8 medium muffin cups. With a rotary beater, beat eggs lightly. Add the remaining ingredients and beat just until smooth. *Do not overbeat.*

Fill the custard cups ½ full, muffin cups ¾ full. Bake 20 minutes, then reduce oven temperature to 350° and bake 15 to 20 minutes longer or until a deep golden brown. Immediately remove from cups.

6 TO 8 POPOVERS.

Three pointers to help you get high-as-the-sky popovers like these every time: **1.** Don't overbeat the batter. **2.** Make sure the oven temperature is on target. **3.** Use deep custard cups for a really spectacular pop-up.

SOUTHERN BUTTERMILK BISCUITS

2 cups all-purpose flour*
2 teaspoons sugar
2 teaspoons baking powder
1 teaspoon salt
½ teaspoon soda
⅓ cup shortening
⅔ cup buttermilk

*If using self-rising flour, omit baking powder and salt.

Heat oven to 450°. Measure flour, sugar, baking powder, salt and soda into a bowl. Cut in shortening with a pastry blender until the mixture looks like meal. Stir in almost all the buttermilk until the mixture rounds up into a ball and no dry ingredients remain in the bowl. If the dough is not pliable, add just enough milk to make a soft, puffy, easy-to-roll dough. (Too much milk will make the dough sticky, too little will make the biscuits dry.)

Round up the dough on a lightly floured cloth-covered board and knead lightly 20 to 25 times, about ½ minute. Roll a little less than ½ inch thick and cut with a floured biscuit cutter. Place on an ungreased baking sheet. For crusty sides, place them 1 inch apart; for soft sides; place them close together in an ungreased layer pan. Bake 10 to 12 minutes or until golden brown. Serve hot, with butter and, if you like, honey or jam.

ABOUT 2 DOZEN 1¾-INCH BISCUITS.

CHIVE DINNER MUFFINS

2 cups buttermilk baking mix
2 tablespoons shortening
1 egg
⅔ cup milk or water
¼ cup snipped chives

Heat oven to 400°. Grease 12 medium muffin cups. Mix all ingredients with a fork and beat vigorously ½ minute. Fill the muffin cups ⅔ full. Bake 12 to 15 minutes or until light brown.

12 MUFFINS.

VARIATION

Herb Dinner Muffins: Omit chives and add 1¼ teaspoons caraway seed, ½ teaspoon crumbled leaf sage and ¼ teaspoon nutmeg.

BALLOON BUNS

1 package active dry yeast
¼ cup warm water (105 to 115°)
¾ cup lukewarm milk (scalded then cooled)
¼ cup sugar
1 teaspoon salt
1 egg
¼ cup shortening
3½ to 3¾ cups all-purpose flour*
1 cup sugar
1 tablespoon cinnamon
18 large marshmallows
½ cup butter or margarine, melted

*If using self-rising flour, omit salt.

Marshmallows do such magic things to these sweet rolls that it's easy to understand why we first called them Hocus Pocus Buns. A marshmallow starts out in the middle and, presto, it disappears — melting away to a sugar 'n spice hollow. A treat that's well worth the trick!

Dissolve yeast in warm water. Stir in milk, ¼ cup sugar, the salt, egg, shortening and 1¾ cups of the flour. Beat until smooth. Mix in enough of the remaining flour to make the dough easy to handle.

Turn the dough onto a lightly floured board and knead until smooth and elastic, about 5 minutes. Place in a greased bowl; turn the greased side up. Cover and let rise in a warm place until double, about 1½ hours. (The dough is ready if an indentation remains when touched.)

Punch down the dough and divide in half. Roll each half about ¼ inch thick and cut into nine 3½-inch circles. Mix 1 cup sugar and the cinnamon in a small bowl. Dip each marshmallow into the melted butter, then into the sugar-cinnamon mixture. Wrap a circle of dough around each marshmallow, pinching together tightly at the bottom. Dip in the butter, then in the sugar-cinnamon mixture. Place in greased medium muffin cups. Let rise about 20 minutes.

Heat oven to 375°. Bake 25 to 30 minutes. Serve warm.

1½ DOZEN ROLLS.

1 **package active dry yeast**
¼ **cup warm water (105 to 115°)**
¼ **cup lukewarm milk (scalded then cooled)**
¼ **cup granulated sugar**
½ **teaspoon salt**
1 **egg**
¼ **cup shortening**
2¼ **to 2½ cups all-purpose flour***
½ **cup butter or margarine**
½ **cup brown sugar (packed)**
½ **cup pecan halves**
2 **tablespoons soft butter or margarine**
¼ **cup granulated sugar**
2 **teaspoons cinnamon**

*If using self-rising flour, omit salt.

Learn the ABC's of this adaptable, rich sweet roll dough. From it you can create any number of coffee cakes as well as a kaleidoscope of rolls in all shapes and sizes. We used it to make the Swedish Tea Ring on page 62 and the Hungarian Coffee Cake on page 60.

BUTTERSCOTCH-PECAN ROLLS

Dissolve yeast in warm water. Stir in milk, ¼ cup granulated sugar, the salt, egg, shortening and 1½ cups of the flour. Beat until smooth. Mix in enough of the remaining flour to make the dough easy to handle.

Turn the dough onto a lightly floured board and knead until smooth and elastic, about 5 minutes. Place in a greased bowl; turn the greased side up. (At this point, the dough can be covered and refrigerated at 45° or below for up to 4 days.) Cover and let rise in a warm place until double, about 1½ hours. (The dough is ready if an indentation remains when touched.)

Melt ½ cup butter in a baking pan, 13 x 9 x 2 inches. Sprinkle brown sugar and pecan halves over the butter.

Punch down the dough and roll into a rectangle, 15 x 9 inches. Spread with 2 tablespoons butter. Mix ¼ cup granulated sugar and the cinnamon and sprinkle over the rectangle. Roll up tightly, beginning at the wide side. Pinch the edge of the dough into the roll to seal well; stretch the roll to make even. Cut into 1-inch slices and place slightly apart in the pan. Cover and let rise until double, about 45 minutes.

Heat oven to 375°. Bake 25 to 30 minutes. Immediately invert the pan onto a serving plate. Let the pan remain a minute so the butterscotch can drizzle down over the rolls.

15 ROLLS.

FROSTED ORANGE ROLLS

Dough for Butterscotch-Pecan
Rolls (page 56)
3 tablespoons soft butter or
margarine
1 tablespoon grated orange peel
2 tablespoons orange juice
1½ cups confectioners' sugar

Prepare the dough for Butterscotch-Pecan Rolls. After punching down the dough, roll into a rectangle, 15 x 9 inches. Mix butter, orange peel, orange juice and sugar; spread half the mixture over the rectangle.

Roll up tightly, beginning at the wide side. Pinch the edge of the dough into the roll to seal well; stretch the roll to make even. Cut into 1-inch slices and place slightly apart in a well-greased baking pan, 13 x 9 x 2 inches. Cover and let rise until double, about 45 minutes.

Heat oven to 375°. Bake 25 to 30 minutes. While warm, top the rolls with the remaining orange mixture.

15 ROLLS.

FANCY FRUIT BUNS

1 package active dry yeast
¼ cup warm water (105 to 115°)
½ cup lukewarm milk (scalded
then cooled)
¼ cup sugar
1 teaspoon salt
¼ cup shortening
1 egg
2¼ cups all-purpose flour*
¼ teaspoon mace
½ teaspoon nutmeg
½ cup cut-up candied fruits
¼ cup raisins
¼ cup chopped nuts
Creamy Icing (page 58)

*If using self-rising flour, omit salt.

Dissolve yeast in warm water. Stir in milk, sugar, salt, shortening, egg and 1¼ cups of the flour. Beat until smooth. Mix in the remaining flour, the mace, nutmeg, fruits and nuts. Cover and let rise in a warm place until double, about 1¾ hours.

Beat down the dough and drop by tablespoonfuls about 3 inches apart onto a greased baking sheet. Let rise until double, about 30 minutes.

Heat oven to 400°. Bake about 15 minutes or until golden brown. While warm, drizzle buns with Creamy Icing.

1½ DOZEN BUNS.

1 package active dry yeast
¼ cup warm water (105 to 115°)
¼ cup lukewarm milk (scalded then cooled)
¼ cup sugar
½ teaspoon salt
1 egg
¼ cup shortening
⅓ cup cocoa
2¼ to 2½ cups all-purpose flour*
2 tablespoons soft butter or margarine
¼ cup sugar
1½ teaspoons cinnamon
   Creamy Icing (below)

*If using self-rising flour, omit salt.

CHOCOLATE CINNAMON ROLLS

Dissolve yeast in warm water. Stir in milk, ¼ cup sugar, the salt, egg, shortening, cocoa and 1½ cups of the flour. Beat until smooth. Mix in enough of the remaining flour to make the dough easy to handle.

Turn the dough onto a lightly floured board and knead until smooth and elastic, about 5 minutes. Place in a greased bowl; turn the greased side up. (At this point, the dough can be covered and refrigerated at 45° or below for up to 4 days.) Cover and let rise in a warm place until double, about 1½ hours. (The dough is ready if an indentation remains when touched.)

Punch down the dough and roll into a rectangle, 15 x 9 inches. Spread with butter. Mix ¼ cup sugar and the cinnamon and sprinkle over the rectangle. Roll up, beginning at the wide side. Pinch the edge of the dough into the roll to seal well; stretch the roll to make even. Cut into 1-inch slices and place slightly apart in a greased baking pan, 13 x 9 x 2 inches. Let rise until double, about 45 minutes.

Heat oven to 375°. Bake 25 to 30 minutes. While warm, frost rolls with Creamy Icing.

15 ROLLS.

CREAMY ICING

Mix ¾ cup confectioners' sugar, 1½ teaspoons milk and ¼ teaspoon vanilla until smooth.

SOUR CREAM TWISTS

1 cup dairy sour cream
1 package active dry yeast
¼ cup warm water (105 to 115°)
2 tablespoons butter or margarine, softened
3 tablespoons granulated sugar
1 teaspoon salt
1 egg
3 cups all-purpose flour*
2 tablespoons soft butter or margarine
⅓ cup brown sugar (packed)
1 teaspoon cinnamon
   Creamy Glaze (below)

*If using self-rising flour, omit salt.

As soon as you finish each twist, place it on the baking sheet. Gently press both ends to keep the proper shape.

Heat sour cream *just* to lukewarm. Dissolve yeast in warm water. Stir in sour cream, 2 tablespoons butter, the granulated sugar, salt, egg and 1 cup of the flour and beat until smooth. Mix in the remaining flour until the dough cleans the side of the bowl.

Turn the dough onto a lightly floured board and knead until smooth, about 10 minutes. Place in a greased bowl; turn the greased side up. Cover and let rise in a warm place until double, about 1 hour. (The dough is ready if an indentation remains when touched.)

Punch down the dough and roll into a rectangle, 24 x 6 inches. Brush with 2 tablespoons butter. Mix brown sugar and cinnamon and sprinkle over a lengthwise half of the rectangle. Fold the other half over the sugared half. Cut into 1-inch strips.

Holding the strips at each end, twist in opposite directions. Place 2 inches apart on a greased baking sheet, pressing the ends on the sheet. Cover and let rise until double, about 1 hour.

Heat oven to 375°. Bake 12 to 15 minutes or until golden brown. While warm, frost with Creamy Glaze.

2 DOZEN TWISTS.

CREAMY GLAZE

Mix 1½ cups confectioners' sugar, 2 tablespoons soft butter or margarine, 1½ teaspoons vanilla and 1 to 2 tablespoons hot water until smooth and of spreading consistency.

CINNAMON WHIRLIGIG

Dough for Balloon Buns (page 55)
¼ **cup sugar**
2 **teaspoons cinnamon**

Prepare the dough for Balloon Buns. After punching down the dough, roll into a rectangle, 16 x 8 inches. Mix sugar and cinnamon and sprinkle over the rectangle.

Roll up tightly, beginning at the narrow side. Pinch the edge of the dough into the roll to seal well. Place seam side down in a well-greased loaf pan, 9 x 5 x 3 inches. Let rise until double, about 1 hour.

Heat oven to 375°. Bake 35 minutes or until golden brown. If the loaf is browning too quickly, cover with foil for the last 15 minutes of baking. For a soft, shiny crust, brush the top of the still-hot loaf with butter or shortening; or you can frost the cooled loaf with Creamy Icing (page 58).

HUNGARIAN COFFEE CAKE

Double recipe for Butterscotch-Pecan Rolls dough (page 56)
¾ **cup sugar**
1 **teaspoon cinnamon**
½ **cup finely chopped nuts**
½ **cup butter or margarine, melted**

Prepare the double recipe of dough. After punching down the dough, shape pieces into 1½-inch balls. Mix sugar, cinnamon and nuts in a small bowl. Dip balls in melted butter, then roll in the sugar-cinnamon-nut mixture.

Place a single layer of balls with sides just touching in a well-greased 10-inch tube pan. (If the pan has a removable bottom, line with aluminum foil.) Top with another layer of balls. Let rise until double, about 45 minutes.

Heat oven to 375°. Bake 35 to 40 minutes. (If the top is browning too quickly, cover with foil.) Loosen from pan and immediately invert the pan onto a serving plate. Let the pan remain a minute so the butter-sugar mixture can drizzle down over the coffee cake. To serve, break apart with 2 forks.

Hungarian Coffee Cake

SWEDISH TEA RING

Dough for Butterscotch-Pecan Rolls (page 56)
2 **tablespoons soft butter or margarine**
½ **cup brown sugar (packed)**
2 **teaspoons cinnamon**
½ **cup raisins**
Confectioners' Sugar Icing (page 64)
Walnuts
Candied cherry halves

Prepare the dough for Butterscotch-Pecan Rolls. After punching down the dough, roll into a rectangle, 15 x 9 inches. Spread with butter, then sprinkle with sugar, cinnamon and raisins. Roll up tightly, beginning at the wide side. Pinch the edge of the dough into the roll to seal well; stretch to make even.

With the sealed edge down, shape the roll into a ring on a lightly greased baking sheet. Pinch the ends together. With scissors, make cuts ⅔ of the way through ring at 1-inch intervals. Turn each section onto its side. Let rise until double, about 45 minutes.

Heat oven to 375°. Bake 25 to 30 minutes or until golden brown. While warm, frost the ring with Confectioners' Sugar Icing and decorate with nuts and candied cherry halves.

Three secrets for creating a Swedish Tea Ring as pretty perfect as this:
1. Stretch and shape the ring evenly.
2. Be sure the cuts are the same size all around. **3.** Carefully turn each section on its side.

BUTTER ALMOND COFFEE CAKE

Almond Topping (below)
1 package active dry yeast
¾ cup warm water (105 to 115°)
¼ cup sugar
1 teaspoon salt
1 egg
¼ cup shortening
2¼ cups all-purpose flour*

*If using self-rising flour, omit salt.

A one-bowl-for-everything coffee cake with the alias "Double Quick Coffee Bread." And an appropriate alias it is — beating takes the place of kneading, and no rolling or cutting is necessary. It's fluffier, thinner crusted and more cake-like in texture than its kneaded counterparts.

Prepare the topping. Dissolve yeast in warm water in a large mixer bowl. Add sugar, salt, egg, shortening and 1¼ cups of the flour. Beat 2 minutes on medium speed, scraping the bowl frequently. Mix in the remaining flour until smooth.

Drop the batter by tablespoonfuls onto the Almond Topping in the pan. Cover and let rise in a warm place until double, about 1 hour.

Heat oven to 375°. Bake 30 to 35 minutes or until golden brown. Immediately invert the pan onto a serving plate. Let the pan remain a minute so the topping can drizzle down over the coffee cake.

ALMOND TOPPING

Melt ⅓ cup butter in a baking pan, 9 x 9 x 2 inches. Stir in ½ cup slivered blanched almonds. Heat until the butter foams and the nuts are golden brown. Remove from heat and cool. Stir in 2 tablespoons light corn syrup, ½ cup sugar and ½ teaspoon almond extract. Spread the mixture evenly in the pan.

VARIATION

Butterscotch-Pecan Coffee Cake: Omit Almond Topping. Instead, melt ⅓ cup butter or margarine and ½ cup brown sugar (packed) with 1 tablespoon corn syrup in the baking pan. Sprinkle ½ cup pecans on mixture. (Candied or maraschino cherries can be added, too.) Cool.

BOHEMIAN BRAID

1 package active dry yeast
¼ cup warm water (105 to 115°)
¾ cup lukewarm milk (scalded then cooled)
¼ cup sugar
1 teaspoon salt
1 egg
¼ cup shortening
½ cup raisins
½ cup chopped blanched almonds
1 teaspoon grated lemon peel
⅛ teaspoon mace
3½ to 3¾ cups all-purpose flour*
1 egg yolk
2 tablespoons cold water
Confectioners' Sugar Icing (below)

*If using self-rising flour, omit salt.

Dissolve yeast in warm water. Stir in milk, sugar, salt, egg, shortening, raisins, almonds, lemon peel, mace and 1¾ cups of the flour. Beat until smooth. Mix in enough of the remaining flour to make the dough easy to handle.

Turn the dough onto a lightly floured board and knead until smooth and elastic, about 5 minutes. Place in a greased bowl; turn the greased side up. Cover and let rise in a warm place until double, about 1½ hours. (The dough is ready if an indentation remains when touched.)

Punch down the dough and let rise again until almost double, about 30 minutes.

Divide the dough into 4 equal parts; shape three of the parts into 14-inch strands. Place on a lightly greased baking sheet and braid loosely. Pinch ends together and fold under. Divide the remaining part into 3 pieces and shape each into a 12-inch strand. Braid these strands and place on the large braid. Cover and let rise until double, 45 to 60 minutes.

Heat oven to 350°. Mix egg yolk and cold water and brush on the braids. Bake 30 to 40 minutes or until golden brown. While warm, frost the braid with Confectioners' Sugar Icing and decorate with candied cherries and pecan halves.

CONFECTIONERS' SUGAR ICING

Mix 1 cup confectioners' sugar and about 1 tablespoon milk until smooth.

SOUR CREAM COFFEE CAKE

¾ **cup soft butter**
1½ **cups sugar**
3 **eggs**
1½ **teaspoons vanilla**
3 **cups all-purpose flour***
1½ **teaspoons baking powder**
1½ **teaspoons soda**
¼ **teaspoon salt**
1½ **cups dairy sour cream**
Filling (below)

*If using self-rising flour, omit baking powder, soda and salt.

Heat oven to 350°. Grease a tube pan, 10 x 4 inches, a 12-cup bundt cake pan or 2 loaf pans, 9 x 5 x 3 inches. Combine butter, sugar, eggs and vanilla in a large mixer bowl. Beat on medium speed 2 minutes, scraping the bowl occasionally. (Or beat 300 strokes by hand.) Mix in flour, baking powder, soda and salt alternately with the sour cream.

For a tube or bundt cake pan, spread ⅓ of the batter (about 2 cups) in the pan and sprinkle with ⅓ of the Filling (about 6 tablespoons); repeat 2 times. For loaf pans, spread ¼ of the batter (about 1½ cups) in each pan and sprinkle with ¼ of the Filling (about 5 tablespoons); repeat.

Bake about 1 hour or until a wooden pick inserted in center comes out clean. Cool in pan(s) a few minutes.

FILLING

Mix ½ cup brown sugar (packed), ½ cup finely chopped nuts and 1½ teaspoons cinnamon.

BLUEBERRY BUCKLE COFFEE CAKE

2 **cups all-purpose flour***
¾ **cup sugar**
2½ **teaspoons baking powder**
¾ **teaspoon salt**
¼ **cup shortening**
¾ **cup milk**
1 **egg**
2 **cups fresh blueberries**
Crumb Topping (below)

*If using self-rising flour, omit baking powder and salt.

Heat oven to 375°. Grease a baking pan, 9 x 9 x 2 inches, or a layer pan, 9 x 1½ inches. Blend flour, sugar, baking powder, salt, shortening, milk and egg; beat ½ minute. Carefully stir in blueberries.

Spread in the pan and sprinkle Crumb Topping on the batter. Bake 45 to 50 minutes or until a wooden pick inserted in center comes out clean. Serve warm.

CRUMB TOPPING

Mix ½ cup sugar, ⅓ cup all-purpose flour, ½ teaspoon cinnamon and ¼ cup soft butter.

FRENCH BREAKFAST PUFFS

⅓ cup shortening
½ cup sugar
1 egg
1½ cups all-purpose flour* or
    cake flour
1½ teaspoons baking powder
½ teaspoon salt
¼ teaspoon nutmeg
½ cup milk
½ cup sugar
1 teaspoon cinnamon
½ cup butter or margarine, melted

*If using self-rising flour, omit baking powder and salt.

Heat oven to 350°. Grease 15 medium muffin cups (2¾ inches in diameter). Mix thoroughly shortening, ½ cup sugar and the egg. Stir in flour, baking powder, salt and nutmeg alternately with the milk. Fill the muffin cups ⅔ full. Bake 20 to 25 minutes.

Mix ½ cup sugar and the cinnamon. Immediately after baking, roll hot muffins in melted butter, then in the sugar-cinnamon mixture. Serve hot.

15 PUFFS.

TINY ALOHA PINEAPPLE MUFFINS

2 cups buttermilk baking mix
¼ cup sugar
2 tablespoons soft butter
1 egg
⅔ cup milk
½ cup well-drained crushed
    pineapple
    Thin Icing (below)
    Chopped nuts

Heat oven to 400°. Grease 48 tiny muffin cups. Mix baking mix, sugar, butter, egg and milk with a fork and beat vigorously ½ minute. Fold in pineapple. Fill the muffin cups ⅔ full. Bake 12 to 15 minutes. While warm, frost with Thin Icing and sprinkle with nuts.

48 MUFFINS.

Note: The muffins can also be baked in 12 greased medium muffin cups. Bake 15 to 20 minutes.

THIN ICING

Mix ½ cup confectioners' sugar and 1 tablespoon water until smooth.

VARIATIONS

Banana Muffins: Omit the milk and pineapple and mix in 1 cup mashed very ripe banana.

Coconut Muffins: Omit the pineapple and fold in ½ cup flaked coconut.

DATE-NUT BREAD

1½ cups boiling water
1½ cups cut-up dates
½ cup brown sugar (packed)
1 tablespoon shortening
1 egg
2¼ cups all-purpose flour*
1 teaspoon soda
½ teaspoon salt
1 cup coarsely chopped nuts

*If using self-rising flour, decrease soda to ¼ teaspoon and omit salt.

Pour boiling water over the dates and cool.

Heat oven to 350°. Grease a loaf pan, 9 x 5 x 3 inches. Mix thoroughly brown sugar, shortening and egg. Stir in the date mixture. Mix in flour, soda and salt, then stir in nuts. Spread in the pan. Bake 60 to 70 minutes or until a wooden pick inserted in center comes out clean.

PUMPKIN BREAD

⅔ cup shortening
2⅔ cups sugar
4 eggs
1 can (16 ounces) pumpkin
⅔ cup water
3⅓ cups all-purpose flour*
2 teaspoons soda
1½ teaspoons salt
½ teaspoon baking powder
1 teaspoon cinnamon
1 teaspoon cloves
⅔ cup coarsely chopped nuts
⅔ cup raisins or cut-up dates

*If using self-rising flour, omit soda, salt and baking powder.

Heat oven to 350°. Grease 2 loaf pans, 9 x 5 x 3 inches, or 3 loaf pans, 8½ x 4½ x 2½ inches. Cream shortening and sugar thoroughly. Mix in eggs, pumpkin and water. Blend in flour, soda, salt, baking powder, cinnamon and cloves. Stir in nuts and raisins and spread in the pans. Bake 65 to 70 minutes or until a wooden pick inserted in center comes out clean.

2 LOAVES.

1 package active dry yeast
¼ cup warm water (105 to 115°)
2 eggs
1 cup whipping cream
1 teaspoon vanilla
⅓ cup sugar
3½ cups all-purpose flour*
1 tablespoon baking powder
1 teaspoon salt
¼ teaspoon cinnamon
¼ teaspoon nutmeg

*If using self-rising flour, omit baking powder and salt.

Raised doughnut versus cake doughnut. Which is the best? No need to choose. Our recipe combines the best of the two doughnut worlds. What's more, you can change the shape of this doughnut; cut the rolled dough into a variety of shapes — hearts for Valentine's Day, stars for Christmas.

But what of the doughnut's famous hole? Some give credit to a 19th-century Maine sea captain who had his fill of his mother's soggy-centered fried cakes and testily instructed her to "cut a hole in the middle where it doesn't cook." Others say it all happened much earlier. They tell of a Nauset Indian who playfully shot an arrow right through one of his wife's fried cakes. As she scurried away in fright, she dropped the perforated patty into a kettle of boiling grease. Today, the "missing" hole is as delicious as the ring.

WHIPPED CREAM DOUGHNUTS

Dissolve yeast in warm water. In a small mixer bowl, beat eggs, whipping cream, vanilla and sugar until light and fluffy. Stir into yeast. Mix in the remaining ingredients until the dough is soft and easy to handle.

In a deep fat fryer or kettle, heat fat or oil (3 to 4 inches deep) to 375°. (The fat is hot enough if a 1-inch cube of bread browns in 60 seconds.) Roll the dough about ⅓ inch thick on a lightly floured cloth-covered board and cut with a floured doughnut cutter.

Drop doughnuts into the hot fat and turn as they rise to the surface. Fry until golden brown on both sides, about 2 minutes. Avoid pricking the doughnuts when removing them from the fat. Drain on paper towels. Serve plain, sugared or frosted.

2 DOZEN DOUGHNUTS.

Note: Fry the doughnut "holes" as a special treat for the children.

VARIATIONS

Bear Tracks: Roll the dough ⅓ inch thick on a lightly floured cloth-covered board and cut into strips, 3 x 1 inch. With a sharp knife, make cuts ½ inch apart and halfway through on one side of each strip. Fry as for doughnuts.

Turnabouts: Turn half the dough onto a lightly floured cloth-covered board. Roll into a rectangle, 15 x 5 inches, and cut into twelve 2½-inch squares. Cut a diagonal slit in each square. Draw a corner through the slit and curl back in the opposite direction. Repeat with the other half of the dough. Fry as for doughnuts.

Desserts

BONNIE BUTTER CAKE

⅔ cup butter or margarine,
  softened
1¾ cups granulated sugar
 2 eggs (⅓ to ½ cup)
1½ teaspoons vanilla
 3 cups cake flour or 2¾ cups
  all-purpose flour*
2½ teaspoons baking powder
 1 teaspoon salt
1¼ cups milk
  Egyptian Filling (below)
 1 cup chilled whipping cream
 2 tablespoons confectioners' sugar

*If using self-rising flour, omit baking powder and salt.

Take special note of this rich and unusual filling — we've had raves on it year after year. Some home-testers tell us it's best with a white layer cake; others prefer it as a topping for devils food squares. Still others use it as a filling *and* on top, as we did here with one of our butteriest yellow cakes. How do you cast your ballot?

Heat oven to 350°. Grease and flour 2 layer pans, 9 x 1½ inches. In a large mixer bowl, mix the butter, granulated sugar, eggs and vanilla until fluffy. Beat 5 minutes on high speed, scraping the bowl occasionally. On low speed, mix in flour, baking powder and salt alternately with the milk. Pour into the pans.

Bake 30 to 35 minutes or until a wooden pick inserted in center comes out clean. Cool.

Spread Egyptian Filling between the layers and on top of the cake. In a chilled bowl, beat the whipping cream and confectioners' sugar until stiff; spread on side of cake. Refrigerate cake until serving time.

EGYPTIAN FILLING

⅔ cup half-and-half
⅔ cup sugar
 2 egg yolks, slightly beaten
½ cup cut-up dates
½ teaspoon vanilla
½ cup chopped toasted almonds

Mix half-and-half, sugar, egg yolks and dates in a small saucepan. Cook over low heat, stirring constantly, until slightly thickened — 5 to 6 minutes. Remove from heat and stir in vanilla and nuts. Cool.

Pictured on the preceding page:
Mocha Brownie Torte,
Peach Shortcake Parisienne,
Company Cheesecake

BEST CHOCOLATE CAKE

2 cups all-purpose flour* or
   cake flour
2 cups sugar
1 teaspoon soda
1 teaspoon salt
½ teaspoon baking powder
¾ cup water
¾ cup buttermilk
½ cup shortening
2 eggs (⅓ to ½ cup)
1 teaspoon vanilla
4 ounces melted unsweetened
   chocolate (cool)
   Fudge Frosting (below)

*If using self-rising flour, omit salt and baking powder.

Heat oven to 350°. Grease and flour a baking pan, 13 x 9 x 2 inches, or two 9-inch or three 8-inch round layer pans.

Measure all ingredients except the frosting into a large mixer bowl. Blend ½ minute on low speed, scraping the bowl constantly. Beat 3 minutes on high speed, scraping occasionally. Pour into the pan(s).

Bake oblong 40 to 45 minutes, layers 30 to 35 minutes or until a wooden pick inserted in center comes out clean. Cool; frost with Fudge Frosting.

FUDGE FROSTING

2 cups sugar
¼ cup light corn syrup
½ cup milk
½ cup shortening
2 ounces unsweetened chocolate
¼ teaspoon salt
1 teaspoon vanilla

Combine all ingredients except the vanilla in medium saucepan. Cook over medium heat, stirring constantly, until chocolate is melted and sugar is dissolved. Heat to rolling boil, stirring constantly. Boil rapidly, stirring constantly, 1 minute or to 220° on a candy thermometer. Remove from heat and stir in vanilla.

Place the pan in a bowl of ice and water to cool slightly, about 5 minutes. Beat the frosting until it loses its gloss and is of spreading consistency, about 10 minutes.

1⅔ cups all-purpose flour*
1 cup sugar
1 teaspoon soda
½ teaspoon salt
1 cup water
¼ cup shortening
1 egg
1 teaspoon vanilla
1 cup cut-up dates**
½ cup finely chopped nuts
  Chocolate Chip-Nut Topping
  (right)

*If using self-rising flour, decrease soda to ¼ teaspoon, omit salt and use 2 eggs.

**Packaged chopped dates (sugar coated) can be substituted for the cut-up dates.

1 package (8 ounces) dried apricots (about 2 cups)
1 package (8 ounces) pitted dates (1½ cups)
¾ pound whole Brazil nuts (1½ cups)
1 cup drained red and green maraschino cherries
⅓ pound red and green candied pineapple, cut up (about 1 cup)
¾ cup all-purpose flour*
¾ cup sugar
½ teaspoon baking powder
½ teaspoon salt
3 eggs (½ to ⅔ cup)
1½ teaspoons vanilla

*If using self-rising flour, omit baking powder and salt.

DATE CAKE

Heat oven to 350°. Grease and flour a baking pan, 9 x 9 x 2 inches. Measure all ingredients except the topping into a large mixer bowl. Blend ½ minute on low speed, scraping the bowl constantly. Beat 3 minutes on high speed, scraping occasionally. Pour into the pan and sprinkle Chocolate Chip-Nut Topping on batter. Bake 45 to 50 minutes or until a wooden pick inserted in center comes out clean.

CHOCOLATE CHIP-NUT TOPPING

Mix ½ cup semisweet chocolate pieces, 2 tablespoons sugar and ½ cup finely chopped nuts.

JEWELED FRUITCAKE

Heat oven to 300°. Line a loaf pan, 9 x 5 x 3 or 8½ x 4½ x 2¼ inches, with aluminum foil, then grease the foil. Leaving the apricots, dates, nuts and cherries whole, mix all ingredients thoroughly. Spread the mixture evenly in the pan.

Bake 1 hour 45 minutes or until a wooden pick inserted in center comes out clean. If necessary, cover with aluminum foil for the last 30 minutes of baking to prevent excessive browning. Remove from pan and cool. Wrap the fruitcake in plastic wrap or aluminum foil and store in a cool place.

ANGEL FOOD DELUXE

1 cup cake flour
1½ cups confectioners' sugar
12 egg whites (1½ cups)
1½ teaspoons cream of tartar
¼ teaspoon salt
1 cup granulated sugar
1½ teaspoons vanilla
½ teaspoon almond extract

Heat oven to 375°. Blend flour and confectioners' sugar and set aside. (For easy blending, sift the flour and confectioners' sugar together.) Measure egg whites, cream of tartar and salt into a large mixer bowl. Beat on medium speed until foamy. Add granulated sugar, 2 tablespoons at a time, beating on high speed until the meringue holds stiff, glossy peaks.

Gently fold in flavorings. Sprinkle the flour-sugar mixture, ¼ cup at a time, over meringue, folding in gently just until the flour-sugar mixture disappears. Carefully push the batter into an ungreased tube pan, 10 x 4 inches. Gently cut through batter with a rubber scraper to break air holes.

Bake on lowest rack 30 to 35 minutes or until a deep golden brown and the top springs back when touched lightly with finger. Immediately invert the tube pan on a funnel and let hang until the cake is completely cool, at least 2 hours.

ANGEL ALEXANDER

Angel Food Deluxe (above)
2 tablespoons half-and-half
½ cup dark crème de cacao
1½ cups chilled whipping cream
¼ cup confectioners' sugar

Bake the cake as directed. Cool in the pan.

Several hours before serving, combine half-and-half and crème de cacao. With a 5-inch wooden skewer, make many holes of varying depths in the cake. Pour half the crème de cacao mixture into the holes; let cake stand in pan 2 hours.

Invert cake onto serving plate. Make more holes in top and pour in remaining crème de cacao.

In a chilled bowl, beat whipping cream and sugar just until stiff; frost side and top of cake. Refrigerate cake until serving time.

3 eggs (½ to ⅔ cup)
1 cup granulated sugar
⅓ cup water
1 teaspoon vanilla
1 cup cake flour or ¾ cup
   all-purpose flour*
1 teaspoon baking powder
¼ teaspoon salt
   About ⅔ cup jelly or jam
   Confectioners' sugar

*If using self-rising flour, omit baking powder and salt.

OLD-FASHIONED JELLY ROLL

Heat oven to 375°. Line a jelly roll pan, 15½ x 10½ x 1 inch, with aluminum foil or waxed paper, then grease. In a small mixer bowl, beat eggs until very thick and lemon colored, about 5 minutes. Pour eggs into a large mixer bowl and gradually beat in granulated sugar. On low speed, blend in water and vanilla. Gradually add flour, baking powder and salt, beating just until the batter is smooth. Pour into the pan, spreading the batter into the corners.

Bake 12 to 15 minutes or until a wooden pick inserted in center comes out clean. Loosen cake from the edges of the pan immediately and invert on a towel that's generously sprinkled with confectioners' sugar. Carefully remove the foil. Trim off the cake's edges if they're very crisp so that it will not split when rolled.

While hot, carefully roll cake *and towel* from narrow end. Cool on a wire rack at least 30 minutes. Unroll cake and remove towel. Beat jelly with fork just enough to soften; spread over cake. Roll up and sprinkle with confectioners' sugar.

10 SERVINGS.

VARIATIONS

Cream Roll: Omit the jelly. In a chilled bowl, beat 1 cup chilled whipping cream and 2 tablespoons confectioners' sugar until stiff. Spread on unrolled cake. Serve roll with sweetened sliced fresh strawberries or peaches.

Ice-cream or Sherbet Roll: Omit the jelly. Slightly soften 1 pint of your favorite ice cream or sherbet and spread on unrolled cake. Freeze roll several hours or until firm.

A cake roll in the old-time tradition . . .
awhirl with a sparkling jelly and sprinkled
with confectioners' sugar.

1. In order to roll the cake easily, it must
be hot. And don't forget the towel — it
keeps the cake from sticking together.
2. Unroll the cooled cake carefully so it
doesn't crack; immediately spread it with
jelly and reroll.

PASTRY

FOR 9-INCH ONE-CRUST PIE

1   cup all-purpose flour*
½   teaspoon salt
⅓   cup plus 1 tablespoon shortening
2   to 3 tablespoons cold water

FOR 9-INCH TWO-CRUST PIE

2   cups all-purpose flour*
1   teaspoon salt
⅔   cup plus 2 tablespoons shortening
4   to 5 tablespoons cold water

*If using self-rising flour, omit salt. Pie crusts made with self-rising flour differ in flavor and texture from those made with plain flour.

The proof of the pie is in its pastry. Get your pie-time off to a perfect start with these pointers:

1. Before you start rolling the dough, cover the board with a pastry cloth and the rolling pin with a stockinet. Sprinkle both with flour and rub it in well.

2. Roll the dough lightly, always working from the center to the outer edge. Roll evenly in all directions, but never back and forth. Lift the pin as you near the edge to keep the dough from becoming too thin.

3. As you roll, keep the outer edge in a circular shape by pushing in gently with slightly cupped hands.

4. To prevent sticking, lift the pastry from time to time. And, when necessary, rub a little more flour into the cloth and stockinet.

Measure flour and salt into a bowl. Cut in shortening thoroughly with a pastry blender. (The particles should be the size of tiny peas.) Sprinkle in the water, 1 tablespoon at a time, tossing with a fork until all flour is moistened and dough almost cleans the side of the bowl (1 to 2 teaspoons water can be added if needed).

Gather the dough into a ball, then shape into a flattened round on a lightly floured cloth-covered board. (For a Two-crust Pie, divide the dough in half and shape into 2 flattened rounds.) Roll the dough 2 inches larger all around than the inverted pie pan.

Fold the pastry into quarters; unfold and ease into the pan, gently pressing toward the center with your fingertips. (This procedure helps prevent the dough from stretching, which would eventually cause shrinkage.)

For One-crust Pie: Trim the overhanging edge of pastry 1 inch from rim of pan. Fold and roll pastry under, even with the pan, and flute. Fill and bake as directed in recipe.

For Baked Pie Shell: Prick bottom and side thoroughly with a fork. Bake in a 475° oven 8 to 10 minutes.

For Two-crust Pie: Pour desired filling into the pastry-lined pie pan. Trim the overhanging edge of pastry ½ inch from rim of pan. Roll the second round of dough. Fold into quarters and cut slits. (The slits allow steam to escape while the pie bakes.) Place over the filling and unfold. Trim the overhanging edge of pastry 1 inch from rim of pan. Fold and roll the top edge under the lower edge, pressing on the rim to seal; flute.

FRESH BERRY PIE

Lattice Top Pastry (below)
1 cup sugar
⅓ cup all-purpose flour
4 cups fresh berries (raspberries, blackberries, boysenberries, loganberries)
1 tablespoon lemon juice
2 tablespoons butter or margarine

Heat oven to 425°. Prepare the pastry. Stir together sugar and flour and mix lightly with the berries. Pour into the pastry-lined pie pan. Sprinkle with lemon juice and dot with butter.

Cover with lattice top; seal and flute. Cover the edge with a 2- to 3-inch strip of aluminum foil to prevent excessive browning; remove the foil for the last 15 minutes of baking. Bake 35 to 45 minutes or until the crust is golden brown. Serve warm.

LATTICE TOP PASTRY

Prepare pastry as directed for 9-inch Two-crust Pie (page 76) except — leave a 1-inch overhang on the lower crust. After rolling the circle for the top crust, cut into 10 strips, about ½ inch wide. For fancy edges, cut the strips with a pastry wheel.

Place 5 strips about 1 inch apart across the filling in the pie pan. Weave a cross-strip through the center by first folding back every other one of the original strips. Continue weaving until the lattice is complete, folding back the alternate strips each time a cross-strip is added. (Too time-pressed to weave? Simply lay the second set of strips across the first set.) Trim ends of strips.

Fold the trimmed edge of the lower crust over the ends of the strips, building up a high edge. (A juicy fruit pie is more likely to bubble over when topped by a lattice than when the juices are held in by a top crust — so be sure to build up a high edge.) Seal and flute.

VARIATION

Blueberry Pie: Decrease sugar to ½ cup, add ½ teaspoon cinnamon and use 4 cups fresh blueberries.

For an even lattice, fold back every other one of the original strips; then weave the cross-strips, handling the center one first.

APPLESCOTCH PIE

5 cups thinly sliced pared tart
   apples (about 4 medium)
1 cup brown sugar (packed)
¼ cup water
1 tablespoon lemon juice
¼ cup all-purpose flour
2 tablespoons granulated sugar
¾ teaspoon salt
1 teaspoon vanilla
3 tablespoons butter or margarine
   Pastry for 9-inch Two-crust Pie
   (page 76)

Combine apple slices, brown sugar, water and lemon juice in a saucepan. Cover and cook over medium heat until the apples are *just* tender, about 5 minutes.

Mix flour, granulated sugar and salt and stir into apple mixture. Cook, stirring constantly, until the syrup thickens — about 2 minutes. Remove from heat and stir in vanilla and butter.

Heat oven to 425°. Prepare the pastry. Turn the apple mixture into the pastry-lined pie pan. Cover with top crust which has slits cut in it; seal and flute. Cover the edge with a 2- to 3-inch strip of aluminum foil to prevent excessive browning; remove the foil for the last 15 minutes of baking. Bake 40 to 45 minutes or until the crust is golden brown.

FRENCH APPLE PIE

   Pastry for 9-inch One-crust Pie
   (page 76)
¾ cup sugar
¼ cup all-purpose flour
½ teaspoon nutmeg
½ teaspoon cinnamon
   Dash of salt
6 cups thinly sliced pared apples
   (about 5 medium)
   Crumb Topping (below)

Heat oven to 425°. Prepare the pastry. Stir together sugar, flour, nutmeg, cinnamon and salt; mix lightly with the apples. Pour into the pastry-lined pie pan and sprinkle with Crumb Topping.

Cover the edge with a 2- to 3-inch strip of aluminum foil to prevent excessive browning; remove the foil for the last 15 minutes of baking. Bake 40 to 50 minutes. If the topping is browning too quickly, cover it with foil for the last 15 minutes of baking.

CRUMB TOPPING

Mix 1 cup all-purpose flour,* ½ cup firm butter or margarine and ½ cup brown sugar (packed) with a fork or pastry blender until crumbly.

*Do not use self-rising flour in this recipe.

CHERRY PIE

Pastry for 9-inch Two-crust Pie
(page 76)
1 ⅓ cups sugar
⅓ cup all-purpose flour
2 cans (16 ounces each) pitted
    red tart cherries, drained
¼ teaspoon almond extract
2 tablespoons butter or margarine

Heat oven to 425°. Prepare the pastry. Stir together sugar and flour and mix lightly with the cherries. Pour into the pastry-lined pie pan. Sprinkle fruit with almond extract and dot with butter.

Cover with top crust which has slits cut in it; seal and flute. Cover edge with 2- to 3-inch strip of aluminum foil to prevent excessive browning; remove the foil for the last 15 minutes of baking. Bake 35 to 45 minutes or until the crust is golden brown and the juice begins to bubble through the slits. Serve slightly warm.

VARIATION

Fresh Cherry Pie: Substitute 4 cups fresh red tart cherries, washed and pitted, for the canned cherries.

CHERRY-BANANA PIE

9-inch Baked Pie Shell
(page 76)
1 can (16 ounces) pitted red
    tart cherries
1 cup sugar
3 tablespoons cornstarch
1 tablespoon butter or margarine
½ teaspoon cinnamon
1 teaspoon almond extract
2 medium bananas

Bake the pie shell. Cool.

Combine cherries (with liquid), sugar and cornstarch in a saucepan. Cook over medium heat, stirring constantly, until the mixture thickens and boils. Boil and stir 1 minute. Stir in butter and cool.

Stir in cinnamon and almond extract. Slice bananas into the pie shell. Pour the cherry filling over the banana slices and chill at least 3 hours or until set. Garnish with whipped cream and banana slices.

BANANA CREAM PIE

9-inch Graham Cracker Crust
  (page 84)
⅔ cup sugar
¼ cup cornstarch
½ teaspoon salt
3 cups milk
4 egg yolks, slightly beaten
2 tablespoons butter or margarine
1 tablespoon plus 1 teaspoon
   vanilla
2 large bananas
   Sweetened whipped cream

Bake the Graham Cracker Crust. Cool.

Mix sugar, cornstarch and salt in a saucepan. Blend milk and egg yolks; gradually stir into the sugar mixture. Cook over medium heat, stirring constantly, until the mixture thickens and boils. Boil and stir 1 minute. Remove from heat and blend in butter and vanilla. Press plastic wrap onto filling in saucepan and cool to room temperature.

Slice bananas into the crust, arranging them in a layer about ½ inch deep. Pour the cream filling over banana slices and chill at least 2 hours. Just before serving, top pie with sweetened whipped cream.

CHOCOLATE PECAN PIE

Pastry for 9-inch One-crust Pie
   (page 76)
1¼ cups light corn syrup
½ cup sugar
1 bar (4 ounces) sweet cooking
   chocolate
½ cup evaporated milk
3 eggs, slightly beaten
1 cup pecan halves

Heat oven to 350°. Prepare the pastry. Combine corn syrup, sugar, chocolate and milk in a saucepan. Heat, stirring constantly, *just* until the chocolate is melted. Gradually stir the hot mixture into eggs, then stir in pecan halves. Pour into the pastry-lined pie pan. Bake 50 to 60 minutes. (Center will appear soft.) Cool. Try this pie topped with sweetened whipped cream or vanilla ice cream.

Note: You'll want to cut this pie into smaller-than-average wedges — it's very rich.

DIVINE LIME PIE

4 egg whites
¼ teaspoon cream of tartar
1 cup sugar
4 egg yolks
¼ teaspoon salt
½ cup sugar
⅓ cup fresh lime juice (2 to 3 limes)
2 to 3 drops green food color
1 cup chilled whipping cream
1 tablespoon grated lime peel

Heat oven to 275°. Generously butter a 9-inch pie pan. In small mixer bowl, beat egg whites and cream of tartar until foamy. Beat in 1 cup sugar, 1 tablespoon at a time, and continue beating until stiff and glossy — about 10 minutes. *Do not underbeat.*

Pile into the pie pan, pressing meringue up against the side. Bake 1 hour. Turn off the oven; leave meringue in oven with the door closed 1 hour. Remove from oven and cool.

Beat egg yolks until light and lemon colored. Stir in salt, ½ cup sugar and the lime juice. Cook over medium heat, stirring constantly, until the mixture thickens — about 5 minutes. Cool and tint with food color.

In a chilled bowl, beat whipping cream until stiff. Fold in the lime mixture and grated lime peel. Pile into the meringue shell and chill at least 4 hours. Garnish with whipped cream and grated lime peel or lime twists.

PINEAPPLE MALLOW PIE

9-inch Graham Cracker Crust (page 84)
32 large or 3 cups miniature marshmallows
1 can (20 ounces) crushed pineapple, drained (reserve ½ cup syrup)
1 cup chilled whipping cream
1 teaspoon vanilla
¼ teaspoon salt

Bake the Graham Cracker Crust. Cool.

Heat marshmallows and reserved pineapple syrup over low heat, stirring constantly, until marshmallows are melted. Chill until thickened.

In a chilled bowl, beat whipping cream until stiff. Stir the marshmallow mixture until blended and fold into the whipped cream. Reserving ½ cup crushed pineapple for a garnish, fold the remaining pineapple, the vanilla and salt into the marshmallow mixture. Pour into the crust and garnish with the reserved pineapple. Chill 2 to 3 hours.

9-inch Baked Pie Shell
    (page 76)
1½ **cups sugar**
 ⅓ **cup plus 1 tablespoon**
    cornstarch
1½ **cups water**
 3 **egg yolks, slightly beaten**
 3 **tablespoons butter or margarine**
 2 **teaspoons grated lemon peel**
 ½ **cup lemon juice**
 2 **drops yellow food color, if**
    desired
    Pie Meringue (below)

There's no mystery to making a perfect meringue pie. With a little care and these clues, the delicate topping will be light-as-air, high and golden brown every try.

1. Separate eggs carefully. (It's easier to do when they're cold.) Even a speck of yolk can hold down the peaks.

2. Wait until the egg whites come to room temperature before beating. They'll be higher and lighter.

3. Beat in the sugar *gradually* — and continue beating until it is completely dissolved.

4. Spread the meringue over a *hot* filling, right to the crust all the way around.

5. Watch baking time.

6. Dodge drafts; a chill may make the meringue shrink.

LEMON MERINGUE PIE

Bake the pie shell. Cool.

Heat oven to 400°. Mix sugar and cornstarch in a medium saucepan. Gradually stir in water. Cook over medium heat, stirring constantly, until the mixture thickens and boils. Boil and stir 1 minute.

Gradually stir at least half the hot mixture into the egg yolks; blend into the hot mixture in the saucepan. Boil and stir 1 minute. Remove from heat and stir in butter, lemon peel, lemon juice and food color. Immediately pour into the pie shell.

Heap the meringue onto the hot pie filling and spread over the filling, carefully sealing the meringue to the edge of the crust to prevent shrinking or weeping. Bake about 10 minutes or until a delicate brown. Cool gradually to prevent shrinking.

PIE MERINGUE
 3 **egg whites**
 ¼ **teaspoon cream of tartar**
 6 **tablespoons sugar**
 ½ **teaspoon vanilla**

Beat egg whites and cream of tartar until foamy. Beat in sugar, 1 tablespoon at a time, and continue beating until stiff and glossy. *Do not underbeat.* Beat in vanilla.

VARIATION

Lime Meringue Pie: Decrease cornstarch to ⅓ cup and omit butter. Substitute 2 teaspoons grated lime peel and ¼ cup lime juice for the lemon peel and juice and green food color for the yellow.

Lemon Meringue Pie

FRENCH STRAWBERRY GLACÉ PIE

9-inch Baked Pie Shell (page 76)
6 cups fresh strawberries (about 1½ quarts)
1 cup sugar
3 tablespoons cornstarch
½ cup water
1 package (3 ounces) cream cheese, softened

Bake the pie shell. Cool.

Mash enough strawberries to measure 1 cup. Mix sugar and cornstarch in a saucepan; stir in water and the crushed berries. Cook over medium heat, stirring constantly, until the mixture thickens and boils. Boil and stir 1 minute. Cool.

Beat cream cheese until smooth and spread on the bottom of the baked pie shell. Fill the shell with the remaining berries and pour the cooked berry mixture on top. Chill at least 3 hours or until set. If you like, serve with sweetened whipped cream.

FROSTY PUMPKIN PIE

9-inch Graham Cracker Crust (below)
1 cup canned pumpkin
½ cup brown sugar (packed)
½ teaspoon salt
½ teaspoon cinnamon
½ teaspoon ginger
¼ teaspoon nutmeg
1 quart vanilla ice cream, slightly softened
Sweetened whipped cream
Walnut halves or candy corn

Bake the Graham Cracker Crust. Cool.

Beat pumpkin, sugar, salt and spices until smooth. Stir in ice cream. Pour into the crust and freeze at least 8 hours. For easy cutting, remove the pie from the freezer 15 minutes before serving. Garnish with sweetened whipped cream and the walnut halves.

9-INCH GRAHAM CRACKER CRUST

1½ cups graham cracker crumbs (about 20 crackers)
3 tablespoons sugar
⅓ cup butter or margarine, melted

Heat oven to 350°. Mix cracker crumbs, sugar and butter. (If desired, reserve 2 to 3 tablespoons crumb mixture to sprinkle on pie.) Press the remaining mixture firmly and evenly against bottom and side of a 9-inch pie pan. Bake 10 minutes. Cool.

BROWNIES

4 ounces unsweetened
    chocolate
⅔ cup shortening
2 cups sugar
4 eggs
1 teaspoon vanilla
1¼ cups all-purpose flour*
1 teaspoon baking powder
1 teaspoon salt
1 cup chopped nuts

*If using self-rising flour, omit baking powder and salt.

Heat oven to 350°. Grease a baking pan, 13 x 9 x 2 inches. Melt chocolate and shortening in a large saucepan over low heat. Remove from heat and mix in the sugar, eggs and vanilla. Stir in the remaining ingredients. Spread in the pan.

Bake 30 minutes or until the brownies start to pull away from the sides of the pan. Do not overbake. Cool slightly. Cut into bars, about 2 x 1½ inches. For a change, spread brownies with Fudge Frosting (page 71) or dust with confectioners' sugar before cutting.

32 BARS.

VARIATION

Peanut Butter Brownies: Decrease shortening to ¼ cup and omit the nuts. Stir in ¼ cup peanut butter and ½ cup chopped peanuts.

LEMON-COCONUT SQUARES

1 cup all-purpose flour*
½ cup butter or margarine,
    softened
¼ cup confectioners' sugar
2 eggs
1 cup granulated sugar
½ teaspoon baking powder
¼ teaspoon salt
2 teaspoons grated lemon
    peel, if desired
2 tablespoons lemon juice
½ cup flaked coconut

*If using self-rising flour, omit baking powder and salt.

Heat oven to 350°. Mix thoroughly flour, butter and confectioners' sugar. Press evenly in an ungreased baking pan, 8 x 8 x 2 inches, building up a ½-inch edge. Bake 20 minutes.

Beat remaining ingredients except the coconut until light and fluffy, about 3 minutes. Stir in coconut and spread the mixture on the hot crust. Bake about 25 minutes longer, just until no impression remains when touched lightly in the center. Cool and cut into squares.

25 SQUARES.

Note: If you like, the coconut can be omitted.

CANDY CANES

½ cup butter or margarine, softened
½ cup shortening
1 cup confectioners' sugar
1 egg
1½ teaspoons almond extract
1 teaspoon vanilla
2½ cups all-purpose flour*
1 teaspoon salt
½ teaspoon red food color
½ cup crushed peppermint candy
½ cup granulated sugar

*If using self-rising flour, omit salt. If using quick-mixing flour, stir 2 tablespoons milk into the butter mixture.

Heat oven to 375°. Mix thoroughly butter, shortening, confectioners' sugar, egg, almond extract and vanilla. Blend in flour and salt. Divide the dough in half and blend food color into one half.

For each candy cane, shape 1 teaspoon of dough from each half into a 4-inch rope. (For smooth, even ropes, roll the dough back and forth on a lightly floured board.) Place the ropes side by side and press together lightly; twist. Place on a greased baking sheet and curve the top of each twist to form the handle of the cane.

Bake about 9 minutes or until set and very light brown. Mix candy and granulated sugar; sprinkle on the hot cookies and remove from the baking sheet.

ABOUT 4 DOZEN COOKIES.

Start a new Christmas tradition in your house with these cheery cookie canes. For the best shape and easiest twisting, press the ropes together lightly.

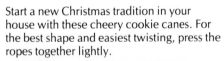

RUSSIAN TEACAKES

1 cup butter or margarine,
  softened
½ cup confectioners' sugar
1 teaspoon vanilla
2¼ cups all-purpose flour*
¼ teaspoon salt
¾ cup finely chopped nuts

*Do not use self-rising flour in this recipe.

Heat oven to 400°. Mix thoroughly butter, sugar and vanilla. Work in flour, salt and nuts until the dough holds together. Shape the dough into 1-inch balls and place them on an ungreased baking sheet.

Bake 10 to 12 minutes or until set but not brown. While warm, roll in confectioners' sugar. Cool and roll in sugar again.

ABOUT 4 DOZEN COOKIES.

BONBON COOKIES

½ cup butter or margarine,
  softened
¾ cup confectioners' sugar
1 tablespoon vanilla
  Food color, if desired
1½ cups all-purpose flour*
⅛ teaspoon salt
  Dates, nuts, semisweet
  chocolate pieces and candied
  or maraschino cherries
  Icing (below)

*Do not use self-rising flour in this recipe.

Heat oven to 350°. Mix thoroughly butter, sugar, vanilla and a few drops of the food color. Work in flour and salt until the dough holds together. (If the dough is too dry, mix in 1 to 2 tablespoons half-and-half.)

Mold the dough by tablespoonfuls around a date, nut, chocolate piece or cherry. Place about 1 inch apart on an ungreased baking sheet. Bake 12 to 15 minutes or until set but not brown. Cool. Dip the tops of the cookies into the icing. Cookies can be decorated with coconut, chopped nuts, colored sugar, chocolate pieces or chocolate shot.

ABOUT 2 DOZEN COOKIES.

ICING

Mix 1 cup confectioners' sugar, 2½ tablespoons half-and-half and 1 teaspoon vanilla until smooth. If desired, stir in a few drops of food color.

DELUXE SUGAR COOKIES

1 cup butter or margarine,
   softened
1½ cups confectioners' sugar
1 egg
1 teaspoon vanilla
½ teaspoon almond extract
2½ cups all-purpose flour*
1 teaspoon soda
1 teaspoon cream of tartar
   Granulated or colored sugar

*If using self-rising flour, omit soda and cream of tartar.

Mix thoroughly butter, confectioners' sugar, egg, vanilla and almond extract. Blend in remaining ingredients except the granulated sugar. Cover the dough and chill 2 to 3 hours.

Heat oven to 375°. Divide the dough in half. Roll each half about ⅛ inch thick on a lightly floured cloth-covered board. Cut into desired shapes and sprinkle with granulated sugar. Place on a lightly greased baking sheet. Bake 7 to 8 minutes or until light brown on the edges. Immediately remove the cookies from the baking sheet.

ABOUT 5 DOZEN COOKIES.

CREAM WAFERS

1 cup soft butter
⅓ cup whipping cream
2 cups all-purpose flour
   Granulated sugar
   Creamy Filling (below)

Mix thoroughly butter, whipping cream and flour. Cover the dough and chill at least 1 hour.

Heat oven to 375°. Using about a third of the dough at a time, roll ⅛ inch thick on a lightly floured cloth-covered board and cut into 1½-inch rounds. With a spatula, transfer the rounds onto a piece of heavily sugared waxed paper. Turn to coat both sides with sugar.

Place the rounds on an ungreased baking sheet and prick each several times with a fork. Bake 7 to 9 minutes or just until set but not brown. Cool; put cookies together in pairs with Creamy Filling.

ABOUT 5 DOZEN COOKIES.

CREAMY FILLING

Mix ¼ cup soft butter, ¾ cup confectioners' sugar and 1 teaspoon vanilla until smooth and fluffy. Tint with food color. If necessary, add a few drops of water for proper spreading consistency.

SALTED PEANUT CRISPS

1 cup shortening (part soft
  butter)
1½ cups brown sugar (packed)
2 eggs
2 teaspoons vanilla
3 cups all-purpose flour*
1 teaspoon salt
½ teaspoon soda
2 cups salted peanuts

*If using self-rising flour, omit salt and soda.

Heat oven to 375°. Mix thoroughly shortening, brown sugar, eggs and vanilla. Stir in the remaining ingredients.

Drop the dough by rounded teaspoonfuls about 2 inches apart onto a lightly greased baking sheet. Flatten dough with the bottom of a glass that's been greased and dipped in sugar. Bake 8 to 10 minutes or until golden brown. Immediately remove the cookies from the baking sheet.

ABOUT 6 DOZEN COOKIES.

VARIATION

Chocolate Chip Peanut Crisps: Stir in 1 package (6 ounces) semisweet chocolate pieces with the salted peanuts.

OLD-FASHIONED OATMEAL COOKIES

1 cup raisins
1 cup water
¾ cup shortening
1½ cups sugar
2 eggs
1 teaspoon vanilla
2½ cups all-purpose flour*
1 teaspoon soda
1 teaspoon salt
1 teaspoon cinnamon
½ teaspoon baking powder
½ teaspoon ground cloves
2 cups oats
½ cup chopped nuts

*If using self-rising flour, omit soda, salt and baking powder.

Simmer raisins and water over medium heat until the raisins are plump, about 15 minutes. Drain raisins, reserving the liquid. Add enough water to the reserved liquid to measure ½ cup.

Heat oven to 400°. Mix thoroughly shortening, sugar, eggs and vanilla. Blend in the reserved raisin liquid. Stir in the remaining ingredients.

Drop the dough by rounded teaspoonfuls about 2 inches apart onto an ungreased baking sheet. Bake 8 to 10 minutes or until light brown. Immediately remove the cookies from the baking sheet.

ABOUT 6½ DOZEN COOKIES.

1 package (15 ounces) fudge
  brownie mix
¼ cup water
¼ cup salad oil
2 eggs
½ cup finely chopped nuts
1½ cups chilled whipping
  cream or 3 cups frozen
  whipped topping*
⅓ cup brown sugar (packed)
1 tablespoon powdered instant
  coffee
  Shaved chocolate or chocolate
  curls

*If using frozen whipped topping, thaw; omit sugar and fold in the instant coffee.

MOCHA BROWNIE TORTE

Heat oven to 350°. Grease and flour 2 layer pans, 9 x 1½ inches. Blend brownie mix (dry), water, oil and eggs. Stir in nuts. Spread in the pans and bake 18 to 20 minutes. Remove layers from pans and place on wire racks to cool thoroughly.

In a chilled bowl, beat whipping cream until it begins to thicken. Gradually add sugar and coffee; continue beating until stiff. Fill layers with 1 cup of the whipped cream mixture. Frost sides and top with the remaining whipped cream mixture and garnish the top with shaved chocolate. Chill at least 1 hour before serving.

10 TO 12 SERVINGS.

PEACH SHORTCAKE PARISIENNE

Heat oven to 400°. Prepare Regular Shortcake dough as directed on a package of buttermilk baking mix except — divide the dough in half and roll one half into a 8-inch square. Place in an ungreased baking pan, 8 x 8 x 2 inches. Dot with butter and sprinkle with ¼ cup brown sugar (packed).

Roll the remaining dough into an 8-inch square and place over the square in the pan. Bake 10 to 15 minutes or until golden brown.

Cut the warm shortcake into squares and serve with sweetened whipped cream or dairy sour cream and sliced fresh or frozen (thawed) peaches.

9 SERVINGS.

COMPANY CHEESECAKE

1¼ cups graham cracker crumbs (about 16 crackers)
2 tablespoons sugar
3 tablespoons butter or margarine, melted
2 packages (8 ounces each) plus 1 package (3 ounces) cream cheese, softened
1 cup sugar
2 teaspoons grated lemon peel
¼ teaspoon vanilla
3 eggs
1 cup dairy sour cream, Cherry Glaze (below) or Strawberry Glaze (below)

Heat oven to 350°. Mix cracker crumbs, 2 tablespoons sugar and the butter. Press the crumb mixture firmly and evenly in the bottom of a 9-inch springform pan. Bake 10 minutes. Cool.

Reduce the oven temperature to 300°. Beat cream cheese in a large mixer bowl. Gradually add 1 cup sugar, beating until fluffy. Add lemon peel and vanilla. Then beat in eggs, one at a time. Pour over the crumb mixture.

Bake 1 hour or until the center is firm. Cool to room temperature. Spread with sour cream or one of the glazes. Chill at least 3 hours. Before serving, loosen edge of cheesecake with knife and remove the side of the pan.

12 SERVINGS.

CHERRY GLAZE

Drain 1 can (16 ounces) pitted red tart cherries, reserving liquid. Add enough water to the reserved cherry liquid to measure 1 cup. Mix ½ cup sugar and 2 tablespoons cornstarch in a small saucepan; stir in the 1 cup cherry liquid. Cook, stirring constantly, until the mixture thickens and boils. Boil and stir 1 minute. Remove from heat. Stir in the cherries and a few drops of red food color. Cool thoroughly.

STRAWBERRY GLAZE

Mash enough fresh strawberries to measure 1 cup. Mix 1 cup sugar and 3 tablespoons cornstarch in a small saucepan. Stir in ⅓ cup water and the strawberries. Cook, stirring constantly, until the mixture thickens and boils. Boil and stir 1 minute. Cool thoroughly.

Steamed Plum Pudding

STEAMED PLUM PUDDING

1 cup milk
3 cups soft bread crumbs
½ cup shortening, melted
½ cup molasses
1 cup all-purpose flour*
1 teaspoon soda
1 teaspoon salt
2 teaspoons cinnamon
¼ teaspoon allspice
¼ teaspoon ground cloves
½ cup cut-up raisins
½ cup finely cut-up citron
  Amber Sauce (below) or
  Sherried Hard Sauce (below)

*If using self-rising flour, decrease soda to ½ teaspoon and omit salt.

The original English "Christmas pudding" — a holiday tradition that dates back to the 1700's — usually included raisins, which at the time were called plums. Thus the dessert came to be called "Plum Pudding."

For this up-to-date version, we ignited warm brandy and then poured it over the pudding. Another method calls for soaking small sugar cubes in lemon extract and placing them around the unmolded pudding. Light just one cube, then stand back and watch the flames encircle the pudding. Whichever method you use, one thing is sure: For the ultimate in drama, out with the lights.

Serve this time-honored dessert with an old Yorkshire adage: "In as many homes as you eat plum pudding in the 12 days following Christmas, so many happy months will you have during the year."

Generously grease a 4-cup mold. In a large bowl, pour milk over bread crumbs and mix in shortening and molasses. Stir in remaining ingredients except the sauce. Pour into the mold and cover tightly with aluminum foil.

Place a rack in a Dutch oven about 1 or 2 inches from the bottom. (If the rack is not adjustable, simply balance it on 2 inverted custard cups.) Pour in boiling water up to the level of the rack and place the filled mold on rack. Heat to boiling. Cover and keep water boiling over low heat 3 hours or until a wooden pick inserted in center of pudding comes out clean. (If more water is needed during the steaming period, lift lid and quickly add boiling water.) Unmold the pudding and cut into slices. Serve warm with one of the sauces.

6 TO 8 SERVINGS.

AMBER SAUCE

1 cup brown sugar (packed) or
  granulated sugar
½ cup light corn syrup
¼ cup butter or margarine
½ cup half-and-half

Mix all ingredients in a small saucepan. Cook over low heat 5 minutes, stirring occasionally. Serve warm.

SHERRIED HARD SAUCE

In a small mixer bowl, beat ½ cup soft butter on high speed until very creamy, fluffy and light in color — about 5 minutes. Gradually beat in 1 cup confectioners' sugar until smooth. Blend in 1 tablespoon sherry or brandy. Chill about 1 hour.

6 egg whites
½ teaspoon cream of tartar
¼ teaspoon salt
1½ cups sugar
2 cups chilled whipping cream
2 packages (3 ounces each)
   cream cheese, softened
½ cup sugar
1 teaspoon vanilla
2 cups miniature marshmallows
   Cherry-Berry Topping (below)

CHERRY-BERRIES ON A CLOUD

Heat oven to 275°. Butter a baking pan, 13 x 9 x 2 inches. In a large mixer bowl, beat egg whites, cream of tartar and salt until foamy. Beat in 1½ cups sugar, 1 tablespoon at a time, and continue beating until stiff and glossy. *Do not underbeat.* Spread in the pan. Bake 1 hour. Turn off the oven; leave meringue in oven with the door closed 12 hours or longer.

In a chilled bowl, beat whipping cream until stiff. Blend cream cheese, ½ cup sugar and the vanilla. Gently fold the whipped cream and marshmallows into the cream cheese mixture; spread over the meringue. Chill 12 to 24 hours. Cut into serving pieces and top with Cherry-Berry Topping.

12 TO 15 SERVINGS.

CHERRY-BERRY TOPPING

Stir together 1 can (21 ounces) cherry pie filling, 1 teaspoon lemon juice and 2 cups sliced fresh strawberries or 1 package (16 ounces) frozen strawberries, thawed.

Is it any wonder that this show-off special never fails to wow guests? And the do-ahead feature makes it especially great for entertaining. Tangy cream cheese, whipped cream, marshmallows and the meringue base mellow together as the dessert chills.

Index